"Oscar Wilde once famously noted: 'I don't want to be at the mercy of n [...] them, to enjoy them, and to dominate them.' Many of us struggle with our [...] us, and sometimes even dominate us. *The Emotional Intelligence Skills Workbook* provides practical, insightful, and effective tools to help you accept and even enjoy your emotions while communicating and connecting with others."

—**Stefan G. Hofmann, PhD**, Alexander von Humboldt Professor at the University of
Marburg, Germany; and author of several books, including *Emotion in Therapy*

"We have all seen those powerful individuals who engage with a clear compass and skillful navigation of interpersonal tensions. Their emotional intelligence is not innate—it can be learned! Stephanie Catella and Matthew McKay have brought together the essential, evidence-based skills that will empower you to lead with your values and communicate effectively, especially when emotions run high. A must-read for anyone wanting to hone their emotional intelligence."

—**Victoria Lemle Beckner, PhD**, associate clinical professor in the department of
psychiatry at the University of California, San Francisco; and coauthor of *Conquering
Post-Traumatic Stress Disorder*

"This book is a research-informed *emotional gift* to the field. Like beloved friends, Catella and McKay take us by the hand and guide us through a journey of exploring the landscape and functions of our emotions, and ways we may surf their waves. With helpful metaphors, playful comments, and a deep sense of kindness, we are skillfully led to explore and act consistently with what matters most."

—**Jennifer Block-Lerner, PhD**, associate professor and PsyD program director at
Kean University, and coeditor of *The Mindfulness-Informed Educator*

"Catella and McKay have created a masterful resource that recontextualizes emotional experiencing in ways that motivate all of us to want to embrace, rather than avoid, painful feelings. Written in practical terms and replete with relatable examples, this workbook is a must-have for anyone who has been overcome by intense emotions and wants to learn new ways of managing them as a path to living a connected, values-driven life."

—**Rochelle I. Frank, PhD**, assistant clinical professor of psychology at the University
of California, Berkeley; and coauthor of *The Transdiagnostic Road Map to Case Formulation
and Treatment Planning*

"In this powerful workbook, Catella and McKay provide you with the knowledge and tools you need to live a life filled with emotions without letting your emotions run your life. By bringing awareness to your emotional world, developing skills to manage your emotions, and embracing a values-driven life, you will improve your communication and strengthen your relationships."

—**Michelle Skeen, PsyD**, psychologist; and author of several self-help books,
including *Love Me, Don't Leave Me* and *Why Can't I Let You Go?*

"*The Emotional Intelligence Skills Workbook* is needed now more than ever. What a better world it would be if we all took the time to listen, be fully present, show empathy, and grow our emotional intelligence. When you use emotional intelligence, the benefits return to you exponentially. Ted Lasso quoted Walt Whitman in saying, 'Be Curious, not Judgmental' about others—this workbook will help you get there."

—**Ken Schlechter**, organizational change management specialist; founder of
Kenneth Michael Consulting Services, LLC; and graduate adjunct professor in
organizational behavior and business ethics at the University of Dayton

"As adults, there's an expectation for us to skillfully grasp, navigate, and express our emotions—yet many of us lack explicit guidance on handling our emotions, particularly when they become distressing. Catella and McKay have gifted us with a user-friendly instruction manual on how to make our emotions work for us instead of against us. *The Emotional Intelligence Skills Workbook* uses evidence-based tools to assist readers in living their values and communicating their needs even when faced with intense emotions. Anyone who experiences emotions will benefit from this resource!"

—**Robyn L. Gobin, PhD**, licensed psychologist; associate professor at University of
Illinois at Urbana-Champaign; and author of several self-help books, including
The Self-Care Prescription

THE
EMOTIONAL INTELLIGENCE SKILLS
WORKBOOK

IMPROVE COMMUNICATION AND BUILD STRONGER RELATIONSHIPS

STEPHANIE CATELLA, PSYD
MATTHEW McKAY, PHD

New Harbinger Publications, Inc.

Publisher's Note

This publication is designed to provide accurate and authoritative information in regard to the subject matter covered. It is sold with the understanding that the publisher is not engaged in rendering psychological, financial, legal, or other professional services. If expert assistance or counseling is needed, the services of a competent professional should be sought.

NEW HARBINGER PUBLICATIONS is a registered trademark of New Harbinger Publications, Inc.

New Harbinger Publications is an employee-owned company.

Copyright © 2024 by Stephanie Catella and Matthew McKay
New Harbinger Publications, Inc.
5720 Shattuck Avenue
Oakland, CA 94609
www.newharbinger.com

Cover design by Sara Christian

Acquired by Jennye Garibaldi

Edited by Karen Levy

Printed in the United States of America

26   25   24

10   9   8   7   6   5   4   3   2   1   First Printing

For every client I've worked with, you have been my greatest teachers
in the artistic expression of evidence-based therapy.

—Steph

For my dear friend, Rich Gosse, who has both supported me
and kept me laughing for sixty years.

—Matt

Contents

Foreword

What would the human experience be without emotion? As I consider this question and drop into the benefits of human connection and being socially oriented beings, it is difficult to imagine a world without expressing our inner selves through emotion. As a species, we would be worse off for its absence. Beautiful and agonizing moments would lose their importance. Empathizing with another's pain would disappear. Running from danger would cease to exist. Love would dissolve. In recognizing this reality, we can learn to appreciate the wisdom and gift of emotion.

Even though I have worked as a psychologist for many years, I am still surprised when clients arrive at my office asking me to help them stop feeling. Of course, this request is typically about specific types of emotion, such as pain, fear, and anxiety. And, given our social context, which often tells us that these experiences are negative or "bad," this request makes sense. These emotions can feel big and, at times, overwhelming. We can respond to our feelings in ineffective and even harmful ways. However, it doesn't mean the request is a good idea. These experiences are a natural part of being alive. We were built to feel emotions, even the ones we don't like.

Three key points have led me to take such an approach to emotional experiencing that is inclusive, broad, and open, allowing all that we feel to be a part of life. First, imagine the loss of someone whom you care deeply about. In this circumstance, what if you could feel no pain? I would argue that you would lose the caring. Indeed, it might no longer matter that they were lost. It is the emotion that signals you care. The feeling connects you to this individual and lets you be touched by their absence. Imagine the loss of joy at the sight of a hummingbird or puppy. Imagine the loss of fear or excitement at the presence of a lion or the prospect of entering a dark cave. It seems easy in these circumstances to appreciate the significance of feeling. Yet, we spend too much time running, hiding from, and fighting our own emotional experience, feeling out of control when emotions seem to hijack or overtake how we want to behave. We turn against ourselves for being human.

Second, when we run from pain, we also run from joy. It is challenging and time-consuming, if not impossible, for humans to excise certain emotions. Suppose we are trying not to feel specific emotions like sadness and anxiety. In that case, we might try to suppress or control them somehow. Interestingly enough, this very effort, because we cannot selectively rid ourselves of a particular feeling, also means we cut ourselves off from joy and happiness. We must shut it all down, become empty or numb, to not feel negative emotions. If we must not have pain, we will surely not have joy.

Third, emotions are the glue of connection and social experience. We begin the connection process from the moment we are born (perhaps earlier). It is done through tears and laughter. It is done through fear and awe. We relate to each other inside of a pool of emotional experiences. They envelope our joining. They structure our social world. This is our gift. This is our promise of love.

All this said, I turn to my deep appreciation of *The Emotional Intelligence Skills Workbook*. Drs. Stephanie Catella and Matt McKay have created a self-help book that guides the reader through a process of opening to, allowing, and responding to feelings in ways that are not only effective but also bring us back to a sense of belonging and connection through the very human and complex experience called emotion. They invite the reader back to emotional awareness, eschewing the social notion that emotions are the enemy. They summon us back to the promise that emotional experiencing holds—belonging and connection.

Drs. Catella and McKay take the reader on a journey, helping them be mindfully present to experiencing emotions in the here and now while connecting with others in meaningful and lasting ways. The journey includes building awareness of internal emotional experiences, sensations, thoughts, and urges; learning to communicate emotions effectively; clarifying personal values and their relevance to emotion; and doing experiential exercises designed to build a flexible relationship with our internal world and the world around us. Ultimately, the skills learned by engaging in the practices in this book chaperone the individual into the wisdom and gift of feeling—into the foundational corners of human connection. I am grateful for this workbook and believe it will assist all who trek through its pages.

—Robyn D. Walser, PhD

CHAPTER 1

Understanding Emotional Intelligence

Have you ever noticed that when you're consumed by an intense emotion, it can be hard to think, listen, or problem solve? In those moments, you've been hijacked by your feelings. *Emotional hijacking* is a natural reaction that occurs when your emotions have taken over and they're calling the shots. When your emotions are consuming, they can cloud your judgment and lead you to say things you regret, jump to conclusions, use a tone of voice that's problematic, storm off in anger, or do a variety of other things that can strain your relationships or make it difficult to create new ones. When we're emotionally hijacked, we're stuck in a loud emotion. It's like having the volume set too high on your headphones and you can't turn it down; it's all you can hear, and it distracts from other things going on within and around you. This is especially common during a challenging conversation, particularly with someone or about something you deeply care about.

It's natural to feel strong emotions in the conversations that matter most to us. Having strong emotions is actually *not* the problem. To the contrary, emotions can provide vital messages about our values, needs, and interests. Yet if we allow feelings to overpower us, they can stand in the way of what we want or need, and our relationships with other people and ourselves can suffer. Living a meaningful life requires the willingness to have some hard conversations and feel the emotions that come along with them. This book was created to help you have those tough talks effectively, no matter how difficult the situation or topic may be. Our goal is to help you build the relationships you want. Before we deep dive into what emotional intelligence is, let's get more specific about what emotional hijacking entails.

The Challenge: Emotional Hijacking

Your body is equipped with a natural response to intense emotions and stressors called fight, flight, or freeze. In the face of high levels of distress, such as an argument with your spouse, feeling misunderstood by your boss, or a hurtful remark from a friend, your nervous system turns on this fight-flight-or-freeze mode in an effort to protect you from the stressor.

In fight mode, your body will prepare you to defend yourself, verbally or physically, which can sometimes look like lashing out at others or getting defensive. In flight mode, your body might send you rapid signals to quickly remove yourself from the stressful situation. This can show up as quickly leaving the room, hanging up the phone abruptly, or canceling something you'd planned to attend at the last minute. In freeze mode, you might feel frozen and immobilized, unsure of what to say or unable to move, as your body's signals send messages of system overload. Freezing can also look like shutting down, taking in very little information during an interaction, and having difficulty finding the words to respond. These are automatic, natural responses that are outside of your control, at least initially.

Although this natural nervous system mechanism was originally designed to protect you, it can sometimes fire too often, turn on its sirens too loudly, or misinterpret the reality of the stressor and turn on when you don't actually need it. Those are times when you've been emotionally hijacked.

The Solution: Emotional Intelligence

As you surely know, emotional hijacking is an intense experience. It can be hard to imagine a conversation going well when you're concerned you'll be in the grip of strong feelings. But another way is possible. Once you're aware of your fight-flight-or-freeze reactions, you can then learn how to respond to them effectively. The key is emotional intelligence.

But what is emotional intelligence? And how do you build it? *Emotional intelligence* (EI) is the ability to experience and accept emotions as they are in the moment, while interacting with others skillfully. With emotional intelligence, you can effectively manage your emotions, notice others' emotions, and have a meaningful and thoughtful conversation, and you do those things simultaneously, even if that conversation is difficult. Put simply, EI involves managing emotional discomfort while communicating skillfully and adjusting your communication approach to suit the context. This may sound complicated, but rest assured, EI is a skill you can learn. You can get better at it, even in a short period of time, and you can measure it to track your progress over time (Mattingly and Kraiger 2019).

Built on the pioneering work of David Sluyter and Peter Salovey (1997) and Daniel Goleman (1995), emotional intelligence is distinct from intellectual abilities, what we commonly term intelligence quotient, or IQ for short. Western cultures often overemphasize intellectual abilities or IQ while failing to teach emotional intelligence. This can leave us lacking some crucial skills for life, especially as a social species. Daniel Goleman explains the problem well: "As we all know from experience, when it comes to shaping our decisions and our actions, feeling counts every bit as much—and often more—than thought. We have gone too far in emphasizing the value and import of the purely rational—of what IQ measures—in human life. For better or worse, intelligence can come to nothing when the emotions hold sway" (Goleman 1995, 4). Intellect is insufficient when navigating strong emotions and the complexities of life; that is where EI is needed.

How Emotional Intelligence Will Help You

Emotional intelligence has been a buzzword since the 1990s, and for good reason. It serves as a glue that bonds our social species together—it helps us collaborate, communicate, coexist, and learn from each other, as well as grow as individuals. We need it to thrive in life, no matter our occupation, social status, personality, or interests.

Let's nerd out for a bit and look at what decades of EI research shows. EI is associated with better physical and emotional health (Schutte et al. 2007; Martins, Ramalho, and Morin 2010), and it serves as a buffer against mental health difficulties and thus physical health conditions as well (Mao, Huang, and Chen 2021). Indeed, EI training improves resilience and decreases stress levels. Those with higher EI skills have more social support and are more satisfied with the social support they receive than those with lower EI (Ciarocchi, Chan, and Bajgar 2001). In the context of work, job satisfaction is strongly connected to EI, and the EI of those in leadership positions has a positive impact on job satisfaction of their staff (Wong and Law 2002). This makes sense, as those with higher EI manage conflict at work more effectively and are more resilient in the face of work stress (Vashist, Singh, and Sharma 2018). Contrary to popular belief, EI has been shown to contribute more to work performance than IQ (O'Boyle et al. 2011).

EI helps us navigate challenging social interactions successfully, have stronger relationships, and cope with stress in ways that reduce the likelihood of physical or emotional health issues. It serves as a buffer against stress and helps us maintain good health in the face of stress, much like bumper guards do in bowling. With emotional intelligence, we can more readily bounce back from stress and keep going.

Research has shown time and again that emotional intelligence is an important and invaluable skill for many reasons. Do you want strong social support? Emotional intelligence is for you. Do you want less stress at work? Emotional intelligence can help with that. Are you prone to avoiding conflict but want to stand up for yourself? Do you want to learn how to navigate differences successfully? That's right, emotional intelligence has what you need. Emotional intelligence is certainly not a cure-all or the answer for everything, but it *is* a foundational skill that can benefit every human being. The following worksheet will help you reflect on the high EI people in your life and identify the EI skills you want to develop (you can also download it at http://www.newharbinger.com/52311).

Who Inspires You?

Creating healthy relationships means fostering connection, facilitating change, and staying focused on having an effective or productive conversation, whatever that may mean to you in that context. People who inspire you as great communicators often leave you feeling motivated to do something differently. You might feel a sense of closeness to them even if they're strangers—they magnetically draw you in. They might also be people in your life who communicate in a way that leaves you feeling heard, seen, understood, or appreciated. Taking some time to reflect on who those people are in your life might also help you notice how *you* aspire to be as a communicator.

When you think of someone who's an excellent communicator, who comes to mind? Think of people you know personally and also people you don't know but admire. List a few of these people below.

_____

_____

_____

How do they capture your attention or draw in their audience with inspiration, awe, or wonder? How do they motivate people and promote change and action? How do they listen and ensure others feel heard? Write down what you appreciate about their communication style.

_____

_____

_____

_____

_____

In all of these examples from your life, notice that this person leaves you feeling something positive, even in the face of a difficult topic or during a time of stagnation or conflict. As you reflect on the skills these excellent communicators display, how do *you* want to be seen? Describe that here.

_____

_____

_____

_____

_____

_____

Keep what you wrote on this worksheet close in mind as you engage with this book. You just noted some important sources of inspiration. You can draw on these to keep you motivated as you learn and apply new skills.

Emotional Gifting

You might be familiar with the terms "emotional vampire" or "drama queen." These kinds of communicators can be draining, causing feelings of disappointment, heaviness, or pessimism. But what is it called when people leave us with a positive feeling after our conversations with them? We call that *emotional gifting*. It's a pleasurable feeling that leaves people wanting to spend more time with someone, connect with them, or get to know them more.

Have you ever had a challenging conversation and found that the other person's response was measured and reasonable, leaving you thinking, *That was easier than I expected?* That's emotional gifting too. Before having what we anticipate will be a difficult conversation, we can reflect on the emotional gift we want to leave the person with. This can help us shift our perspective to *how* we can show up to promote change and facilitate a desire for connection and interaction with this person in the future. The following worksheet will help you reflect on your motivation for enhancing your EI (you can also download it at http://www.newharbinger.com/52311).

Your Emotional Intelligence Motivators

When first learning a new approach, it can be worthwhile to reflect on what you'd like to achieve and uncover some of your motivations for embarking on change. What's the main emotional experience you want people to have after a difficult conversation with you?

_____

_____

What do you hope being more emotionally intelligent will do for you? What do you want to gain from developing this skill? For example, you may hope to understand your kids better, get a promotion, or learn how to set boundaries.

_____

_____

_____

How do you expect emotional intelligence skills will positively affect your relationships? For example, you may expect to create closeness with your partner, reduce miscommunications at work, or help people get to know you more easily.

_____

_____

_____

_____

Your motivations for buying and working through this book are likely quite personal—they really matter to you. The motivations you identified are here to guide and propel you ahead so you can give the emotional gifts to the people you care about and, importantly, to yourself. Emotional intelligence skills are just as much a benefit to our relationships as they are to us.

Because EI is a skill you'll be building throughout this book, let's get a baseline of your current emotional intelligence level. You'll complete this scale again in the last chapter so you can see the progress you've made and identify any areas for continued growth (you can also download the assessment at http://www.newharbinger.com/52311).

What Is Your EI Baseline?

The items in this scale are different ways of dealing with emotions and conflict with others. Do your best to rate each item in terms of how often you've used the strategy or experienced the difficulty over the past three months. Be sure to choose the most accurate answer for you, rather than thinking about how you want to be perceived.

Rate how often the following statements are true for you, where 0 means almost never and 4 means you use this strategy or have this experience very often.

0	1	2	3	4
Almost Never	Rarely	Sometimes	Often	Very Often

#	Item	0	1	2	3	4
1	It takes a while for me to recover after having strong negative emotions.					
2	I lose control over my emotions with others and lash out or "blow up."					
3	When I find myself in an argument, I am quiet and/or try to get out of it quickly.					
4	I put in a lot of effort to avoid feeling strong emotions.					
5	Disagreeing with others makes me uncomfortable and anxious, so I avoid it.					
6	I often act on my emotions without thinking; I tend to do what they push me to do.					
7	In an argument, I state my case and focus on winning and not losing ground.					
8	If I feel strong negative emotions, I can feel driven to drink, use drugs, and/or cut or hurt myself in some way.					
9	I have to bring up issues with others immediately even if my emotions are still strong.					
10	I avoid asking for what I want or need from others.					
11	I use nicotine, drugs, or alcohol to help change or numb my emotions or distress.					
12	When I'm upset, my behavior gets out of control.					
13	I ignore my own needs to avoid conflict or being seen in a negative way.					
14	My emotions drive my behavior, even if it means I regret it afterward.					

#	Item	0	1	2	3	4
15	I push to get my position across and focus on convincing others to adopt it.					
16	I avoid feeling uncomfortable emotions as much as possible.					
17	If I feel strong emotions (such as shame or anger), I act in ways that hurt me or get me in trouble.					
18	I explore issues in a disagreement and focus on hearing all sides.					
19	I can communicate effectively despite having strong emotions.					
20	I try to give each person, including myself, time to share their concerns.					
21	I adjust my tone of voice and body language to connect with others.					
22	I avoid creating useless tension and focus on what really matters with people.					
23	I think things through before bringing up an issue with someone.					
24	I'm not afraid of having strong emotions and trust that I can recover from them.					
25	I'm aware of my emotions as I experience them and accept them as they are.					
26	I can experience strong emotions and am skilled in managing them.					
27	I know how to adjust what I'm asking for based on who I'm speaking to.					

#	Item	0	1	2	3	4
28	I notice when my tone of voice or body language changes.					
29	I use cues from others to adjust my communication approach.					
30	I know how to develop rapport quickly with someone I'm not familiar with.					
31	I still carry out my responsibilities even if I'm experiencing strong emotions.					
32	I negotiate with others when there is a disagreement and compromise to try to meet each person's needs, including my own.					

Scoring instructions: Reverse score items 1 to 17 such that 4 becomes 0, 3 becomes 1, 2 stays 2, 1 becomes 3, and 0 becomes 4. Score items 18 to 32 as written. Then, add the total points for each column separately. Next, add the totals for each column together to get the total score. Where does your score fall in the ranges below?

0–40: Your emotions often get the better of you and make communication challenging. Keep reading along. You're in the right place at the right time—the skills in this book will help.

41–82: You have moderate EI skills and sometimes have difficulty with strong emotions, emotion avoidance, and/or communicating effectively in the face of uncomfortable emotions. This book can teach you some new skills to add to your repertoire.

83–128: You have moderately high to high EI skills. There's always room to improve or discover new ways to express EI. Keep reading to learn new strategies and road-test them.

Emotion-driven behaviors subscale reprinted with permission from the Comprehensive Coping Inventory–55 (CCI–55) (Zurita Ona 2007; Pool 2021).

Summary

To live the life you want, you'll sometimes need to have hard conversations. The things that matter most to you can also bring up the strongest emotions, so these conversations can be difficult at times. But with the skills of emotional intelligence, you can have those important talks successfully, no matter what emotions come up. This book was created to help you have effective conversations, despite how difficult the context or topic might be, and build the relationships you want.

So far, you've learned three important concepts: emotional hijacking, emotional intelligence, and emotional gifting. In this book, you'll learn several skills to become an expert at emotional intelligence:

1. Developing awareness of your emotions

2. Managing uncomfortable emotions

3. Clarifying your values

4. Communicating skillfully

5. Expressing attunement and empathy

6. Rehearsing difficult conversations to solidify your skills

The skills you'll learn in this book are tried-and-true methods taught in evidence-based therapies, including acceptance and commitment therapy (ACT; Hayes, Strosahl, and Wilson 1999), dialectical behavior therapy (DBT; Linehan 1993), cognitive behavioral therapy (CBT), and emotion efficacy therapy (EET; McKay and West 2016). Together, they offer an effective approach to learning emotional intelligence and deepening your connection to yourself and others.

You likely bought this book with a hope for change. We're here to help you make that change! Reading the words on these pages is a great start. To fully get the hang of EI, you'll also need to put the skills taught in this book into practice, sometimes repeatedly. Learning EI takes patience, repetition, and dedicated practice, but the benefits are worth that price. If that sounds overwhelming or intimidating, that's understandable; just notice that response and let those thoughts go. We've broken down the process of learning EI into manageable steps, and we'll teach them in a sequence you can use for years to come.

The workbook includes worksheets and audio tracks to help you to learn and practice the skills. Many of these materials are available for download at the website for this workbook: http://www.newharbinger.com/52311. See the very back of this workbook for details.

CHAPTER 2

Disentangling from Emotions

We are all born with the ability to develop emotional intelligence. In fact, the human mind and body are hardwired for it. Emotions and how we act on them play a crucial role in how satisfying, close, and connected our relationships are. Watching a young baby, you can see how readily they feel and express strong emotions. This ability is pivotal to thriving, as it communicates basic needs to parents and caregivers. Over the course of childhood and into adulthood, we learn healthy and problematic ways to express, reduce, and avoid emotions. Coupled with explicit teachings to be logical, even in the face of the emotional, emotion data can easily get lost or discarded. The emotional part of the brain is reflexive and reacts faster than the reasonable part of the brain, creating a fast track to repeatedly acting in default ways. But there is another way. You can reverse these unhelpful patterns and retrain the mind and body to experience and manage intense emotions. In doing so, you'll also create space to recognize and respond skillfully to other people's emotions.

Reacting Versus Responding

Reacting looks like this: an uncomfortable emotion, thought, physical sensation, or urge arises, and immediately after, a reaction occurs. Notice there is no space in between them. You experience something and automatically and without thought or consideration, you quickly react. Reactions can be adaptive and serve us well when we're faced with an emergency or need for immediate safety, like if you encountered a bear on a hike. A rapid fight-flight-or-freeze activation of your nervous system aims to protect you. But being reactive to emotions is not adaptive in day-to-day life—it is draining, can leave you reeling from one emotion to the next, and often creates unhealthy relationships with oneself and others.

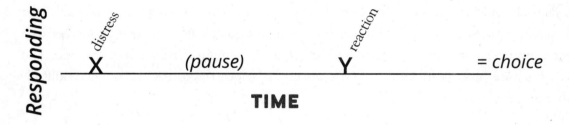

However, a healthy response occurs when there is a pause between the activating event and one's actions. Notice the space between them. A response is considered, thought out, and deliberately chosen, with guidance from your values (what you care about most in life; more on this in chapter 4). It allows you time to reflect on what matters most to you in the moment and/or within that context so you can choose your response accordingly.

Helping you increase the frequency with which you respond rather than react to your emotional experiences is one of the primary goals of this book. We'll teach you how to get there, one chapter at a time.

Emotions Are Empowering

At any given moment, you're feeling at least one emotion. The word "emotion" itself can be confusing. So what exactly are they and why do we have them? Emotions are information signals generated by the mind's observation and interpretation of what's happening within and outside us. Intended to help us make choices, they can serve a variety of purposes. Importantly, emotions:

- Alert us to danger

- Signal we have an unmet need

- Attempt to help us self-protect

- Teach us about ourselves

- Help us understand others

- Facilitate connection with others

- Can reflect our values (what matters most to us)

By decoding your emotions and their purpose, you can choose how best respond to them.

Without full awareness of your inner experience, you're unable to harness your feelings for the clarity they can provide, nor use them to connect with others or express them in healthy ways to communicate. In other words, emotional self-awareness is a foundational requirement of and facilitator to developing emotional intelligence. As you increase your ability to fully experience your emotions without getting hijacked by them, you'll also boost your confidence in managing them, and the urges to avoid them may feel less intense or arise less often.

Sometimes without realizing it, we hold strong beliefs about emotions that shape our reactions to them. Beliefs about emotions can be deliberately or unintentionally adopted through modeling others' behavior, internalizing cultural messages and norms, or responding at times of immense pain, such as a crisis, a traumatic event, or through repeated challenges. Although the mind holds on to these beliefs to try to protect us the next time that emotion arises, it can be negatively biased in its recall of events. Looking within to unearth beliefs at play can empower us to make new choices when they arise. In the following worksheet, you'll reflect on your beliefs about emotions and where those beliefs originated (you can also download it at http://www .newharbinger.com/52311).

Sticky Thoughts About Emotions

Take a few minutes to check in and ask yourself the following questions. The answers are just for you and will help you notice what might show up unannounced as you change your relationship to your emotions.

Growing up, I learned that emotions are: _____

_____

_____

In general, I'd describe my relationship with uncomfortable emotions as (e.g., aversive, distressing, I don't like them and try to avoid them, I work hard to make them go away as quickly as possible):

_____

_____

_____

What do I think it means about me when I have strong and uncomfortable emotions?

_____

_____

_____

I judge myself for what I'm feeling by (e.g., more self-criticism, self-punishment, or self-harm):

_____

_____

_____

_____

It's common for people to judge how they feel, judge themselves for having those feelings, and get caught in a loop of self-criticism. That makes the emotions more painful and creates a belief that feelings are "bad," "to be avoided," or denote something negative about you. Yet, emotions are necessary to communicate and connect with other people, and quite frankly, we need them to survive as a social species.

With clarity on how you currently relate to your emotions, your work is to notice any tightly held negative beliefs and hold them lightly. As you read on, those unhelpful thoughts might pop back up, and that's okay. Let the choices you made to open this book support you. Sometimes discomfort or even initial skepticism can indicate progress—you are indeed doing something different from your default mode. In this chapter, and throughout the book, we'll teach you how to notice your emotions, identify their purpose, and use them to connect and communicate in healthy ways.

Automatic Pilot

Every moment we're awake is a moment of choice. The key is to be present enough to notice those moments of choice. If we habitually live on automatic pilot, we can't see that an opportunity exists. Automatic pilot is a shortcut the mind and body generate when we aren't giving the present moment our full attention. This natural state saves us time and energy, so we tend to use it with ease, particularly during mundane tasks like putting on our shoes or doing the dishes. It allows us to complete tasks without our full attention; we're just going through the motions while conserving energy.

Although automatic pilot has some benefits, it can easily be overused, and that comes with costs. If it is overused or used at the wrong time, we are checked out when we may have actually wanted to be tuned in, like zoning out during a conversation and missing frustration expressed in a loved one's tone of voice. If automatic pilot is a default mode for avoiding emotions, we end up living a limited life dictated by emotions and the strong and rapid reactions they can provoke. For better or worse, what we resist feeling persists. Avoided emotions will remain unresolved and they return to remind us we have unfinished business. This can leave us stuck in cycles of reeling from strong feelings coupled with feeling anxious about them and what might happen next. If we aren't aware of our emotions as they occur and don't allow them to exist, we miss out on an opportunity to respond thoughtfully to them, and we pay the price for this later. When avoidance of emotions is the default mode, over time, the fear of having emotions builds, making emotions scarier and more overwhelming.

With more awareness of our emotions as they occur in real time, we are presented with an opportunity to evaluate our choices and intentionally *choose* a response to our emotions, rather than be bossed around by them. If you could choose what emotions arise, you already would. Just like you can't choose what thoughts pop into your mind, emotions just show up uninvited too. Because no human can control that, you can save energy by allowing what's already there to be and foster a healthy relationship with your inner experiences (it's a whole new world! Cue Disney's *Aladdin*). Who do you want to be in control anyway? You or something you may not have wanted or asked for in the first place? Allowing discomfort to be as it is, you become a sage boss.

The Four Parts of an Emotion

Emotions are complex and travel with an entourage. Every emotion has four components:

1. The emotion itself

2. How it manifests in your body via physical sensations

3. Thoughts that arise with the emotion

4. Urges

Urges, or impulses, can come in two forms: they can tell us to take action or to avoid something. Building full awareness of all four components will increase your understanding of emotions and help you develop a healthy relationship with your inner world. Following is a list of common emotions to help you articulate what you're feeling. Anytime you're unsure what you're experiencing, this list can help.

List of Emotions

Adored	Determined	Fulfilled	Loving	Shy
Afraid	Devastated	Glad	Mad	Skeptical
Amazed	Disappointed	Grateful	Moved	Smart
Angry	Discouraged	Guilty	Nervous	Sorry
Annoyed	Disgusted	Happy	Obsessed	Stimulated
Anxious	Disturbed	Helpless	Optimistic	Strong
Ashamed	Doubtful	Hopeful	Overwhelmed	Surprised
Blessed	Eager	Horrified	Passionate	Suspicious
Blissful	Embarrassed	Hurt	Pleased	Terrified
Bored	Empty	Hysterical	Proud	Thankful
Bothered	Energetic	Impatient	Puzzled	Thrilled
Broken	Enlightened	Indifferent	Regretful	Tired
Bubbly	Enlivened	Infatuated	Relieved	Touched
Cautious	Enraged	Insecure	Reluctant	Trusting
Comfortable	Envious	Inspired	Remorseful	Uncomfortable
Concerned	Excited	Interested	Respected	Unsure
Confident	Exhausted	Irritated	Restless	Upset
Confused	Flirtatious	Jealous	Sad	Vivacious
Content	Foolish	Joyful	Satisfied	Vulnerable
Curious	Fragile	Lively	Scared	Worried
Delighted	Frightened	Lonely	Scattered	Worthless
Depressed	Frustrated	Loved	Secure	Worthy

Let's Try It On

Right about now, you may be thinking, *Emotional intelligence sounds great, but how am I supposed to learn it?* Strong emotions like fear and anger can be truly challenging. It's not always easy to soothe your mind and communicate calmly. But it *is* possible, and we're here to teach you how. To turn down the volume on strong emotions, you have to first notice that you're being hijacked. This means learning to notice your own unique signs that the emotional volume is loud enough to drown out other information. Here's a quick exercise to help you do just that (you can also download it at http://www.newharbinger.com/52311).

═══════ Noticing Emotional Hijacking Cues ═══════

Bring to mind a vivid memory of a time that you "lost it," blew up at someone, said something in anger or frustration, shut down, withdrew, or abruptly removed yourself from a situation. What happened? Write a brief summary, focusing on observable behaviors (what you could see and hear yourself doing).

_____

_____

_____

_____

Notice and name the emotions this experience evoked at the time. You can reference the List of Emotions above to help.

_____

_____

Being careful not to judge yourself, rate how intense that emotion was on a scale of 0 to 10, with 0 being no intensity and 10 being the most intense feeling.

_____

What physical sensations do you remember having at that time? Sometimes these can be hard to notice. If that's the case, close your eyes, put yourself back in this emotionally intense memory, and then scan your body from head to toe and note anything you notice in your body now.

_____

_____

_____

_____

What thoughts did you have during this emotional hijacking? As best you can, write them down verbatim.

_____

_____

_____

_____

What urges or impulses did you have during this emotional hijacking? If you acted on them, how did that go?

_____

_____

_____

_____

Looking back on it now, what are some other perspectives or reasonable factors at play that you couldn't see at the time? (Examples: It was a miscommunication, I was vulnerable to a blowup because I accidentally skipped lunch, I wasn't expecting to have this difficult conversation.)

_____

_____

_____

_____

Despite our best efforts, we all "lose it" sometimes or shut down and withdraw. If you notice your mind is bringing up self-critical or judgmental thoughts, that's okay. Just notice them and let them be. You don't have to do what they say. Reflecting back can help you more readily notice cues leading up to an emotional hijacking or notice that it's already happened and respond accordingly. As you build keen awareness of your emotional experiences, you'll be able to intervene before a default mode kicks in.

Practicing Emotion Awareness

Bolstering awareness of your emotions can take many forms. We'll walk you through some tried-and-true methods to help you foster this skill. You can experiment with them and, over time, you'll figure out which methods work best for you. When developing any new skill, repeated practice and patience are key—be kind to yourself along the way and celebrate your progress so you can see where you're growing and identify areas for improvement. The following worksheet will help you track your emotions on a daily basis (you can also download it at http://www .newharbinger.com/52311).

=== Daily Emotion Log ===

Once daily, log the most intense emotional experience of the day and rate the intensity of the experience, from 0 to 10, with 0 being not intense at all to 10 being the most intense. It might help to do this either in the morning for the day before or several hours before bedtime. Because this could be activating, you'll want to avoid doing it within an hour or two before you go to bed.

Emotion(s)	Physical Sensations	Thoughts	Urges	Intensity (0–10)

Catching Emotion Cues

Often emotions show up in the body first, like a clenched jaw when angry, tears of gratitude, or tightness in the chest when stressed or anxious. By routinely practicing a body awareness exercise, you can catch emotions when they first begin to surface. The following meditation will help you build your emotion awareness muscle and enhance acceptance of whatever your experience is. You can practice it when you're feeling a strong emotion, as well as when you aren't. It can also be useful to notice more "positive" feelings, like contentment, joy, and gratitude—doing so will allow you to more readily notice and maybe even savor them. You can follow along to a guided audio version of this meditation at http://www.newharbinger.com/52311 or make a recording of this on your cellphone.

Body Scan Meditation

Get into a position that works best for you and your body today. Close your eyes if that feels comfortable to you, or softly fix your gaze on the floor.

Just begin by noticing your breath. Follow the movement of the breath as it flows in and out of your body.

With each breath in, see if you can allow the breath to expand deeper in your chest and belly.

With each breath out, allow it to gently leave your chest and belly completely.

Continue breathing deeply while you take an inventory of any emotions you notice now. When you notice one, just name it, and then gently see if there are any others.

If your mind has wandered, that's okay. Bring it back to following the breath, in and out.

Shifting your attention, now take an inventory of your physical sensations. Gently shift your attention to your head and face. Notice the muscles of your forehead, eyes, nose, and jaw.

Just notice any physical sensations as you do this, and let them be there exactly as they are.

And now move your awareness down to your neck and shoulders. Notice sensations there without judging them or yourself.

Gently shift your attention to your chest, stomach, and arms. Note any sensations there and allow them to be as they are.

If you notice sensations you don't like, just note that and allow them to be there. Continue to deeply breathe in and out.

Shift your attention down to your hips, thighs, and bottom. Notice and allow any sensations there.

You don't have to like or want the sensations you notice. They're already there, so just let them be.

And now move your attention to your knees and calves. Note any sensations and use the breath to help you make space for sensations.

If you notice your mind is judging your experience or getting distracted, that's okay. It's what minds do. Just bring your mind back to the breath and then back to your body.

And now shift your attention down to your ankles, feet, and toes. Notice sensations there and allow them to be.

And now expand your awareness to your body as a whole. Just notice what it feels like in this moment without judgment.

Breathe in deeply, and slowly exhale completely.

Rest your attention on the rise and fall of your breath and its rhythm.

Take a moment to congratulate yourself for choosing to be present with your emotions and how they show up in your body.

And now whenever you feel ready, slowly and gently open your eyes.

Observing Emotions in the Moment

Learning how to notice emotions can be hard and humbling work. It takes time and dedicated practice—there's no way around that. But you can quickly build your emotion awareness muscle by tuning in to your emotional experience daily with brief exercises.

Two-Minute Emotion Check-In

Once a day, when you notice an emotion, pause and identify the four components: the emotion itself and accompanying physical sensations, thoughts, and urges. If you have difficulty pausing when you notice emotions, that's okay. Set an alarm on your cellphone or put a specific time in your calendar that is reliably free of distraction and practice this exercise then. Closing your eyes can help you turn your attention inward and name each experience, but you can also do this with your eyes open. This practice is meant to be quick and easily accessible. Consider doing it routinely or when you have time, like while waiting in line somewhere, in between meetings, waiting for your coffee or tea to brew, or during TV commercial breaks.

1. Begin by taking an inventory of the emotions you notice in this moment. Just label them using emotion words without judgment.

2. Notice how those emotions show up in your body. Note and name any physical sensations.

3. Notice the thoughts that accompany your current emotional experience. Just notice them and let them go.

4. Lastly, identify any urges to avoid or act. Just note these and resist doing what the urges say. Simply observe them.

In the beginning, it might be challenging to notice all four components. Just notice what you can and keep deliberately tuning in. With time, you'll build full awareness and quicker access to it. It's not uncommon to get stuck on the thoughts during emotion awareness practices. If you notice that during these emotion check-ins, skip step 3 altogether.

Training the Mind

Learning new skills can at times prompt a mix of emotions: excitement, humility, pride, or frustration, to name a few. There will be inevitable upswings and occasional derailments. Jack Kornfield, a meditation teacher and author, likens developing present moment awareness to training a puppy (Kornfield 1993, 58). The same also applies to learning how to experience and accept emotions: During puppy training, you repeatedly put your puppy down and say, "Sit. Stay." It wanders off in different directions, finds something new to explore or chew on, or runs around. You again say "Stay" and again it gets distracted. Patiently, you say, "Sit. Stay." You don't scream at or hurt the puppy. You keep kindly bringing it back time and time again. Over time, the puppy learns how to sit in stillness.

By repeatedly being gentle with ourselves, we train the mind and body to stay with the present moment and notice our full emotional experience without judgment. Just like the puppy, after a while, the mind settles down and can be steady and stay in the moment, even when it's intense.

Summary

Emotion awareness is an empowering vehicle to emotional intelligence. Wholly coming to know your emotional experience allows you to learn more about yourself and others, harness your emotions to make choices about what matters to you, and connect more deeply with others. Finding comfort in your ability to notice and manage your own emotions will help you become attuned to others' feelings as well. By creating a routine to practice the skills taught in this chapter, you'll foster new emotion acceptance skills to support you on your path to connecting with emotional intelligence.

CHAPTER 3

Riding Emotion Waves

Emotions come in waves. There is a leading edge, they crest, and then they subside in a trailing slope. Even when there is a strong trigger, emotional waves are relatively short-lived (Ekman 1994). In fact, research shows that the average emotion lasts less than 7 minutes. Our subjective sense of how long feelings last, however, may not fit with the research. Painful emotions often seem to go on and on, lasting hours or even days.

There are three things that cause a relatively short emotional surge to stretch out in seemingly endless distress. We can get stuck at the top of an otherwise brief wave by doing one or more of these ineffective coping strategies:

1. *Trying to get rid of the emotion.* This means attempting to ignore, suppress, numb, resist, or in any way block the emotional wave. We now know, from dozens of studies, that trying to suppress emotions makes them worse and longer lasting. The more you try to push emotions away, the more you have them and the longer you remain stuck at the top of the wave.

2. *Thinking about your emotions.* It's natural to wonder where an emotion comes from and seek to explain why you're feeling the way you do. But when you start to ruminate about your feelings and their causes, when you obsess about how bad it would be if the feeling continues, the negative thoughts drive you deeper into the emotions. The thoughts become like a storm wind, blowing up steep waves. And once again you get stuck at the top because rumination keeps the wave from subsiding.

3. *Acting on your emotional urges.* Every emotion is accompanied by an urge to do something. Typical emotion-driven behaviors include *withdrawal* for depression and shame, *aggression* for anger, and *avoidance* for fear and anxiety. Extensive research has confirmed that the more you act on your emotions, and the more those urges shape your behavior, the longer you get caught at the top of the wave (Aldao, Nolen-Hoeksema, and Schweizer 2009; Chawla and Ostafin 2007; Purdon 1999; Sauer and Baer 2009; Selby, Anestis, and Joiner 2008; Wegner et al. 1987). Aggressive speech and behavior beget more anger; withdrawal makes depression worse and prevents us from overcoming shame. Avoidance is the father of anxiety, keeping us scared and running from challenges.

What are the lessons here? Surfing brief emotional waves is far better tolerated than getting stuck at the top. If you can learn to watch your emotions, seeing how they rise and fall without resisting them, the wave is usually short. Even if it's painful, the wave is something you can get through. Further, if you can learn to observe your emotions, without getting caught in "why" thoughts and rumination, the feelings will soften and pass. Finally, when you learn to watch the wave rather than act on emotional urges (withdrawal, aggression, avoidance), then the emotion will gradually diminish.

You always have a choice when feelings are triggered: surf the wave or make it worse.

Emotion Efficacy

Learning how to surf your emotional waves is called emotion efficacy, and emotion efficacy therapy (McKay and West 2016) has been proven effective in multiple studies (Boersma et al. 2019; Abdi Sarkami, Mirzaian, and Abbasi 2020; Sutton-Smolin 2019; Zareie Faskhudi et al. 2021). In this chapter, you'll become an emotion surfer while learning to accept the four parts of an emotional experience:

1. The feelings themselves

2. Sensations in your body

3. Thoughts you can notice and let go of

4. Emotional urges

Obstacles to Surfing and Accepting Emotions

Few people avoid pleasant emotions. If you're having a good time and feeling happy, you probably want more of it. But painful emotions trigger aversion—you want to stop the pain right now. Emotion avoidance takes the three forms just discussed:

- Blocking awareness of the emotion, trying to push it away.

- Trying to figure out where the emotion came from—rumination—in hopes that you can discover ways to control or stop the feeling.

- Acting on emotional urges to get short-term relief (which is what motivates emotion-driven behaviors to begin with) while failing to notice the long-term intensifying effect (stuck at the top of the wave).

The coping strategy of emotion avoidance is the source of chronic emotional pain and emotional disorders. It's understandable that we reflexively try to avoid pain, but it's a habit that must be overcome in order to gain emotion efficacy. Emotion surfing helps you do the exact opposite of emotion avoidance. It teaches you how to watch and accept even the most distressing feelings that arise—so that they will soften and pass, and you can move on to the next experience of the present moment. This next moment will be something different, something that itself will pass and make way for another experience. By observing your feelings, your present moment will keep changing, and even the most difficult emotion will morph into something new.

Exposure: Creating Emotion Acceptance

Emotion exposure involves just one thing: watching your emotions as they arise. But there is a method to exposure. Once learned, it will free you from living at the top of the wave and open up choices to act on what matters most to you.

Building Emotion Awareness

You can learn more about your feelings by inducing them—generating emotional reactions through music or movies. Select some songs or movies that you're familiar with, ones that trigger feelings when you've listened or watched them in the past. Now expose yourself to the emotion by following these steps:

1. Listen or watch attentively, and notice when the emotion starts to show up. Pay close attention to the feeling.

2. Name the emotion. On the worksheet that follows, write as much description as you can about this feeling. You may notice that you're experiencing more than one feeling, or a blend of feelings. Note this down as well.

3. Notice and name any sensations in your body that accompany the emotion. For example, tightness in your chest, a warm feeling in your face, heaviness in your stomach, and so on. Note these on the worksheet.

4. Notice and name any thoughts that show up with the emotion. Write these down verbatim.

5. Notice and name any urges associated with the emotion without acting on them. What does the emotion make you want to do? Write this down on the worksheet.

Repeat this process several times with different songs or movies—ideally ones that trigger different feelings. A sample worksheet is included first, and then you can use the blank one to write your own responses (you can also download them at http://www.newharbinger.com/52311).

Emotion Awareness Worksheet

Julie's Example

Song: "American Idiot" by Green Day

Describe your emotion: Anger, disgust, hopeless feeling, rebellious feeling.
Describe sensations in your body (connected to the emotion): Tightness in stomach, face feels hot, widespread feeling of tiredness in my body.
Describe your thoughts (connected to the emotion): "This country is wrecked...no one to trust...how can I go on living here?"
Describe your action urges (connected to the emotion): Want to yell at my father. Quit my job. Join an activist group.

Song or Movie: _____

Describe your emotion:
Describe sensations in your body (connected to the emotion):
Describe your thoughts (connected to the emotion):
Describe your action urges (connected to the emotion):

Noticing and Accepting How You Feel

The work ahead is to observe and accept feelings in the past, present, and future. In this first section, you'll examine feelings as they show up *now*.

At this very moment you're having emotional experiences. They may be strong or barely noticeable. Regardless, the following exercise will help you practice observation and acceptance of all four parts of your emotional experience. You can follow along to a guided audio version of this at http://www.newharbinger.com/52311 or make your own recording of this on your cellphone.

Guided Mindful Acceptance

Sit comfortably, and either close your eyes or pick a spot to focus on in front of you and relax your gaze.

Now, take a few minutes to notice any sensations in your body. Scan your body until you find a sensation and rest your attention on it. See if you can let it be just as it is and get curious about it. Notice its size and shape, whether it's moving or staying the same, if there's any temperature or tension to it. See if you can soften to it, or even lean into the sensation…

Now, see if you can identify a feeling label that goes with the sensation…just name it and allow it to be as it is without judging or reacting to it.

Next, just notice and watch your thoughts. Our brains produce thoughts all the time, but the key is not to get involved with them. Instead, as each thought arises, you can simply say, "There's a thought," and then let the thought go. Afterward, return to the present moment, and wait for the next thought to arise. Now, for the next few minutes, notice your thoughts.

[Pause]

Next, see if there's an urge that goes with your sensations, feelings, or thoughts. It could be an urge to do something or not do something. Try to just sit with the urge. Notice what it's like not to act on the urge, to just surf it.

[Pause]

Repeat the above sequence.

[Pause]

Take a few deep breaths and slowly open your eyes as you bring your attention back to the room.

Set a goal for listening to the Guided Mindful Acceptance recording four or five times in the next week. Try to make room for each part of your emotional experience. Some emotions may be harder than others to accept, but practicing acceptance increases your awareness and openness to each feeling as it arises.

Emotion surfing is about watching and accepting at the same time. The next exercise shows you how to do it using emotional upsets from the recent past. Acceptance of past discomfort can help us heal from upsets and potentially glean wisdom from them. You can follow along to a guided audio version of this visualization at http://www.newharbinger.com/52311 or make your own recording of this on your phone.

Surfing Feelings from the Past

1. Select an event, the memory of which can still evoke emotion. This shouldn't be overwhelmingly upsetting, but something that triggers a distress level of 5 or 6, on a scale of 0 to 10. It could bring up any emotion, but ideally one you struggle with.

2. Imagine the provoking scene. Try to watch the events unfold—what happened, what was said—as if you were watching a video. Add sounds—voices and what you could hear in the environment. Notice the feel of the environment—the temperature and texture of things you touched. Keep imagining the scene until you've reached a distress level of 5 or 6 (on the 10-point scale). Then cut the scene off; stop the visualization.

3. Now ride the emotional wave:

    •   What's happening in your body? Internally describe any sensations you feel, where they're located, as well as how intensely they affect you. See if you can make room for and accept these sensations.

    •   What's the emotion that goes with that? Name the emotion; try to describe it to yourself with some detail and specificity. For example, if the feeling is on the anger spectrum, is it closer to irritable, enraged, upset, frustrated, disgusted, or annoyed? You don't have to like it or want it, but try to accept this emotion.

    •   Notice how strong the distress level is on a scale of 0 to 10.

    •   Now watch and let go of thoughts. Briefly note the thought(s) that seem to accompany your emotion. Then actively let them go. It might help to take a big breath, and as you exhale just let the thought go with the breath. It's hugely important not to dwell on these thoughts. If you start pursuing emotion-driven thoughts, the emotion will get more intense. Remember, rumination keeps you stuck at the top of the wave. The key is to watch briefly and let go.

- Now observe your action urge. What does this emotion push you to do? Describe it to yourself. Accept the presence of the urge without acting on it.

- Where are you on the wave? Is the emotion getting more intense on the leading edge, are you at the crest, or are you somewhere on the back of the wave where the feeling is subsiding? Just picture where you are on the wave.

- Keep cycling through these observations until (1) the emotion starts to notice-ably subside, or (2) it morphs into a different feeling. With some scenes and emotions, you may only cycle through the process once or twice. With others, you may cycle three to five times until you notice a change.

4. When you finish surfing, determine your distress rating and write down anything you learned. This could be something you learned about the experience of emotion surfing or about your ability to ride the wave.

Utilize your emotion surfing protocol during the next three to four weeks, not with over-whelming triggers, but with events pushing up feelings in the 4 to 6 range. The more you practice surfing, the more confident you'll become that you can accept and tolerate your feelings—and get caught less often at the top of the wave.

Let's see how this works in real life. Here's an example of Lawrence emotion surfing.

Lawrence has been struggling with shame, so he selected a recent event that triggered feelings of inadequacy. There were moments in the past when his shame shot up to 9 or 10 on the 10-point scale, but he chose a scene where the feelings were more moderate (5 to 6).

The triggering scene that Lawrence chose was one where his wife criticized his cooking. Lawrence prides himself on his pasta sauces—and the one that sparked her comments was a Bolognese. He visualized their kitchen—his blue cast-iron pots and the carefully set table. He could see his wife frowning, making little smacking sounds with her mouth. He heard her voice—high and irritated: "You always make this too sweet, Lawrence. I've told you, but you pour the sugar in." He remembers more of the conversation. The television was on in the other room, and he wondered if she'd rather be watching it. He remembers suddenly feeling hot, flushed.

As Lawrence imagines the scene, he notices the beginning of his shame reaction, but keeps visualizing until it's in the 5 to 6 range. At this point, he cuts off images of his wife and the kitchen—and starts to surf the wave. What follows is Lawrence's internal monologue:

- Sensations: *I'm feeling hot in my face, kind of an electric feeling in my chest. A heaviness, like it's hard to move. It's pretty intense, particularly the flushed feeling in my face.*

- Emotions: *Shame. The feeling of not doing things right. Inadequate. A little anxiety about failing (the electric feeling).*

- Rating: *About 6*

- Thoughts: "Why does she have to say that? Even things I think I do right, aren't right." He takes a breath and lets this one go. "She doesn't think much of me." A very sticky thought—he can't seem to let it go. Lawrence shifts attention to urges (so he doesn't make the feeling worse with rumination).

- Action urges: *Get up and leave the table* (what he did at the time). *Just shut down; stop talking to her.*

- Where on the wave: *Climbing toward the top.*

Now Lawrence cycles through his surfing protocol a second time.

- Sensations: *Face still hot—less so. Electric feeling gone. Feel heavier in limbs.*

- Emotions: *Shame. Not really anxious anymore. A small feeling of anger—more like a combination of sorry and annoyed.*

- Rating: *5*

- Thoughts: "I give up." "I can't please her." He takes a breath and lets it go, careful not to stick with these painful thoughts.

- Action urges: *Kind of angrily apologize and withdraw into my take-home work—which annoys her.*

- Where on the wave? *The back end, but still close to the crest.*

Lawrence cycles through again:

- Sensations: *Hot feeling is almost gone; still a bit heavy in legs.*

- Emotion: *Kind of a somber feeling—like this is how it is. But shame is softer, kind of melting into a mild dismay.*

- Rating: *3*

- Thoughts: "I like my sauce; maybe I'll put less sugar in it."

- Action urges: *Tell her I'm cutting sugar.*

- Where on the wave: *Halfway down the back end.*

Because his distress level had decreased noticeably (and the feeling had morphed a bit as well), Lawrence felt ready to stop surfing. He wrote the following about what he'd learned: "I learned, at least at that level (6), I can stand the feeling. And that if I just keep watching, it fades. I also saw how intensely my action urges affect me. I really want to do that stuff. But maybe I have a choice—I'm not sure."

An easy-to-use summary of emotion surfing follows.

Emotion Surfing Steps

Once you're emotionally activated, take note of your distress (0 to 10) level and then begin to practice emotion surfing following the sequence below:

1. Ask yourself, "What sensations do I notice in my body?"

2. Ask yourself, "What's the feeling that goes with it?"

3. Watch and let go of thoughts.

4. Notice urges. Locate the moment of choice instead of acting on the urges.

5. Ask yourself, "Where am I on the wave?" Determine your distress rating.

6. Ask yourself, "What's happening in my body?"

7. Ask yourself, "What's happening to the feeling? Try to allow and make room for that feeling.

8. Watch thoughts and notice urges. Try not to get involved with them.

9. Ask yourself, "Where am I on the wave?"

10. Ask yourself, "What's the sensation in my body?" Try to accept that sensation.

11. Ask yourself, "What's my feeling?" Try to allow and make room for that feeling.

12. Watch thoughts and notice urges. Try not to get involved with them.

13. Ask yourself, "Where am I on the wave?"

14. Keep going until the distress improves or the emotion shifts. Record your distress (0 to 10) level when finished.

Getting Trapped in the Future

Humans can't help peering into the future, trying to anticipate things that may happen and how they'll feel about them. We try to prepare ourselves for negative scenarios, using worry to cope with uncertainty. The result may be to avoid—out of fear, shame, or other painful emotions—things we need to do and that really matter to us.

A better way to prepare for challenging times where emotions are likely to be triggered is to *surf the future*. This is like surfing scenes from the past, but the focus now is on watching and feeling emotions while experiencing urges as a moment of choice—ones on which you don't have to act.

In later chapters of this book, you'll learn to replace action urges with values-based behavior. There will be something you can do to supplant those old emotion-driven behaviors. But right now, while surfing your feelings in the future, the most important thing is to bring your full awareness to the urge—and realize that you can let it determine how you respond, or not.

Exposure: Surfing Your Feelings in the Future

1. Select the future event—something you anticipate could elicit strong emotions. Because it hasn't happened yet, there's no way of gauging how strong your reaction might be. So there's no need to assess a distress level on your 0 to 10 scale.

2. Imagine the scene as it's likely to occur—not the most feared outcome, and not some possible but unlikely scenario. Visualize the people involved; visualize yourself interacting with them. Notice the environment; notice what you hear and physically feel as the scene unfolds. Keep watching until you feel an emotional reaction.

3. Ride the emotional wave.

    • Notice what's happening in your body and describe to yourself what those sensations are like. Where are they? Notice their level of intensity. See if you can accept this experience.

    • Find words to describe the emotion. Be as specific and exact as you can—trying for the description that seems most right. Do your best to make room for and accept the emotion.

    • Note your distress level on a scale of 0 to 10.

    • Now observe your thoughts about the scene. Say to yourself, "I'm having the thought…" and then complete the sentence with your thought. After noticing each thought, take a breath and, as you release it, let the thought go.

    • Now notice the action urge. This is the important part. What does your emotion make you want to do in this future situation? Feel the drive inside to submit to this urge. See exactly what it pushes you to say and how it wants you to react. Notice that this is a moment of choice. Feel the pressure to act. But also observe that there is a choice *not* to engage in old emotion-driven behavior. What would this be like?

    • Where are you on the wave?

4. Keep surfing and cycling through the steps until (1) the emotion feels tolerable and (2) you sense a degree of emancipation from the action urge—you can imagine *not* acting on it. It doesn't seem to drive your behavior in the way it did as you began surfing. By accepting and allowing the emotion, you'll feel less pressure to attack, withdraw, or avoid.

Let's see how this works in real life. Here's an example of Ellie emotion surfing the future.

Ellie wants to talk to her brother regarding her dad's need for assisted living care. Her brother strongly believes her father should remain independent and tends toward anger when discussing the issue. Ellie is afraid of his temper, and at the same time, wants to protect her dad because he's having falls and difficulty managing alone. Ellie keeps putting off the conversation because she worries about how her brother may react.

Ellie began exposing herself to her feelings by imagining a breakfast visit they had scheduled for Saturday. She visualized the restaurant—a pancake place they enjoy. She could see her brother across from her, his face clouding and his voice rising with irritation. He shoves his food away. "There you go again, Ellie, trying to control people." He's getting louder. His hands are in fists, and he looks like he might get up and leave. Ellie imagines her hands on the cold Formica tabletop, trying to keep them steady. She feels the anxiety rise in her chest and shuts off the scene.

Now Ellie starts emotion surfing. What follows is her internal monologue:

- Sensations: *I'm feeling tightness in my chest, cramping in my stomach, a little adrenaline rush. I try to allow the feeling, not fight it.*

- Emotions: *Anxiety. I have a sense that he'll leave and abandon me.*

- Rating: *7*

- Thoughts: "He'll blow up and leave…he thinks I'm a bitch…Dad's helpless, alone in that house." Each thought hits hard, but I know if I get swept up in them, the anxiety will get worse. I'm trying to control my fear by predicting what will happen—I know that doesn't work. I say to myself, "I'm having the thought that…," take a breath, and let it go.

- Action urge: *My urge is to avoid—cancel lunch or say nothing about Dad. And I'm strongly tempted to do one or the other. This will be a moment of choice.*

- Where on the wave: *Right at the top.*

Now Ellie cycles through the surfing protocol again.

- Sensations: *Tightness in chest still, but less. No adrenaline now. Trying to allow the tightness.*

- Emotions: *Still anxious, a little less.*

- Rating: 6

- Thoughts: "I'm having a thought that…maybe he'll leave." "I'm having the thought that…he'll get over it." I take a breath and let it go.

- Action urge: *Plead with him; apologize. This is also strong, but I recognize the choice: to say what I need to say, or back down.*

- Where on the wave: *Just starting down the back of the wave.*

Ellie repeats the surfing protocol twice more until the anxiety is around 4, and she feels firmer in her intention to have the breakfast and ask her brother to help her make a plan— even if they don't do anything just yet.

Emotion Surfing for Emotion Regulation

Emotion surfing is a skill you can use every day—whenever a significant negative emotion threatens to push you into emotion avoidance and get stuck at the top of the wave. The work of surfing is to observe and accept all parts of the emotion, while noting and letting thoughts go.

Emotion surfing is like any new thing you're learning—the more you practice, the more confident you become in your new ability. So start with emotion awareness via music or movies. Then move on to the Guided Mindful Acceptance exercise so you can learn to allow, rather than resist, your feelings. Finally, practice emotion surfing with recent upsets and future challenges.

Summary

After two to four weeks practicing acceptance and emotion surfing, you'll have built significant willingness and commitment to face rather than avoid feelings. You're ready for here-and-now emotion surfing—observing, allowing, and accepting emotions as they occur *in real time*. Now, whenever emotions arise—particularly difficult ones—you can watch and accept them while riding the wave.

CHAPTER 4

Leading with Your Values

As an inherently social species, our world was created on interconnection and the need for collaboration and effective communication. Few humans live, work, or go about life in sustained isolation. As a result, conflict is truly unavoidable. Different ideas will emerge, opposing perspectives will surface, and varying lived experiences will need to be unearthed to deepen empathy, understanding, and collaboration. Emotional intelligence supports us in building meaningful social bonds, maintaining them, and staying connected despite tension or disagreement. To that end, knowing the values you hold dear can provide clarity when communicating and facilitate connection with others.

Can you recall a time you stood up for something or expressed a strongly held belief that didn't align with those around you? What you stood for in that moment was likely your values. Values are the things in life you care about most and how you want to show up in the world. While they can be nouns, like fairness or growth, values must be verbs—they are actions we take, either internally (e.g., how we relate to ourself) or externally (e.g., how we interact with others). Although there are several skills necessary to develop emotional intelligence, values are in essence what keep us anchored in striving for emotional intelligence in the first place. Your values are your why, your motivation, and your fuel to persist, even if honoring them is difficult.

Because values are what you deeply care about, when you act on them, you don't check them off a list and decide you're done caring about them. You keep going. Goals are specific, achievable things you *can* check off a list, such as calling your brother, scheduling a meeting with your team, or presenting at a conference. Values are how you show up as you work on that goal, such as being free of distractions when you call your brother, clearly communicating expectations to your team, or using your tone of voice and body language to engage your audience. You can think of your goals as the destination and your values as the light that guides your way.

Why Values Matter

We all get stuck sometimes, feeling unfulfilled, uninspired, or burnt out. These unavoidable experiences suggest something is missing and not being attended to in life. Discovering our values and honoring them is a way out, and a way toward fulfillment, inspiration, and a more joyful life. They are your guiding light, a reliable compass when you're lost that you can glance at to know which direction to go in.

This can be a new way of making decisions that necessitates repeated practice. When tuning in to your values compass becomes a regular practice, you'll build resilience, confidence, and increased motivation to overcome obstacles. In relationships, honoring your values conveys authenticity to others, which helps foster trusting, lasting relationships and reduces others' uncertainty about where you stand or what you care about most. Being true to your values in your relationships puts others at ease because they can easily detect there's no hidden agenda. Letting your values guide your decisions might sound unfamiliar and maybe even confusing, so let's dig in to what this means a bit more.

Emotion-Driven Behaviors Versus Values-Based Actions

When emotionally hijacked, we engage in what are called emotion-driven behaviors. These are behaviors in which emotions run the show and dictate decision making. This can lead to regret, shame, and other emotional discomfort as well as ruptures and tension in relationships. It can also erode trust that sometimes cannot be repaired. Emotion-driven behaviors can cause bigger problems in the long run, because when you are emotionally hijacked, they tend to carry a compelling, but often biased, message.

Values-based actions, on the other hand, are when emotions are noticed, and attended to, but what determines our actions is thoughtful decision making based on our values. To tune in to values and discover available values-based actions, you can ask yourself, "What do my values tell me to do in this moment?" And notice the difference between that answer and the answer to

"What do my emotions tell me to do?" What your emotions tell you to do is often a reflection of the urges that accompany them (recall the four components of an emotion). Rather than do what emotional urges suggest, instead ask, "What do my values tell me to do?" That is your new guiding compass in life.

One of the underlying goals of this book is to increase values-based action and reduce emotion-driven behavior. Learning this important skill will support you in having emotionally intelligent conversations, no matter the emotional charge they bring.

If acting on values instead of emotions were easy, we'd be unemployed therapists. Avoiding what is uncomfortable is a natural reaction. To increasingly take values-based actions, it's first helpful to know what inevitable barriers might arise along the way. Avoidance of emotions is a barrier to values-based actions and can take many forms:

- Emotion-driven behaviors

- Uncertainty about the future and a desire for clarity

- Procrastination

- Worry

- Rumination

- Distraction

- Avoiding situations, people, or places that prompt strong emotions

- Suppression behaviors (self-harm, substance abuse, withdrawal, etc.)

Each of these barriers is a form of avoidance, as they aim to lessen, eliminate, distract from, or otherwise control an experience of discomfort. Reducing avoidant behaviors is only necessary when avoidance interferes with taking values-based action. Watching your favorite TV show after a stressful day of work may technically be avoidance of the stress and other discomfort, but if doing so doesn't stand in the way of what you value, it isn't problematic avoidance. However, if watching TV meant you canceled plans with a close friend, that would be problematic avoidance because it came at the cost of your values related to the friendship.

You can think of values as different paths you could take on a hike, and emotions as the ever-changing weather. Sometimes honoring your values is easy, like walking the flat hiking trail on a sunny day. Other times, honoring your values is like taking the steep trail when it's pouring rain. Your thoughts, emotions, urges, and physical sensations may not cooperate, but you keep going, even though it's challenging and frustrating and your emotions might be yelling at you to quit. Thankfully, to honor your values, your mind and emotions don't need to fully cooperate—you can keep the unhelpful thoughts, emotions, and urges at bay while you persevere on the trail.

The following exercise will help you clarify your commitment to your values, which will help you persevere when the trail gets steep and rocky (you can also download it at http://www.newharbinger.com/52311).

Reflecting on Your Commitment to Your Values

In this exercise, you'll reflect on a time you deeply cared about something and, despite emotional discomfort and avoidance urges, you stood up for it. You fought for it and committed yourself to honoring your values.

Describe a challenging situation when your values conflicted with someone else's. Identify your values in the situation; be as specific as possible (e.g., integrity, compassion, fairness, honesty). You can review the Common Values list in a later section of this chapter if needed (see page 50).

_____

_____

_____

_____

How did you honor your values during this values conflict? Identify the values-based actions you took (e.g., I stayed calm while saying I disagreed, I listened without interrupting).

_____

_____

_____

_____

What emotions did you experience during this interaction? Review the List of Emotions in chapter 2 if needed (see page 19).

_____

_____

What did you learn you're capable of as a result of honoring your values despite discomfort doing so? (For example, I can effectively assert my opinion even when I'm wound up, I can withhold judgment and criticism when I strongly disagree.) Be as specific as possible.

_____

_____

_____

_____

_____

_____

Recalling times you've honored your values because it was the right thing to do can help bolster confidence that you can do it again, when the time arises. Honoring your values might be difficult at times, but it is worth it to live a life that makes you feel fulfilled.

Values Exploration

You can further explore and reflect on your values in several ways. One approach is to identify the broad categories of life that apply to you and explore your values within each of them. Or you can review a list of values and identify those that resonate most with you. Feel free to try them both out or go with the method that's most appealing. The following daily practice will also help you put your values into action and clarify them.

Keep in mind that your values are solely yours to choose. Values can be influenced by culture, social norms, gender expectations, and upbringing, but also by personal experience and wisdom gleaned from life events. While values can be influenced, you and only you get to decide what you value. When working on the exercises in this chapter, keep this in mind to help you dig deep into what *you* truly hold most dear and set aside the rest. The following worksheet helps you reflect on your values in various domains of life, such as family or education (you can also download it at http://www.newharbinger.com/52311).

Life Domain Values

Choose the domains below that apply to you and rate their importance to you on a scale of 0 to 10, with 0 being not important at all and 10 being extremely important. Then reflect on how you want to show up in that area of your life. Be specific in writing what it would look like to honor your values in each particular area of your life. You can ask yourself, "If someone could observe me honoring my values, what would they see and hear me doing?" Lastly, put a star next to your top three to five domains—these are the areas of your life in which you are the most dedicated and loyal (e.g., your ride-or-die values).

Friends and social life	Rating:
Values:	

Family of origin	Rating:
Values:	

Parenting/co-parenting	Rating:
Values:	

Physical/emotional health	Rating:
Values:	

Self-growth	Rating:
Values:	

Education/learning	Rating:
Values:	

Career/work	Rating:
Values:	

Recreation, hobbies, and fun	Rating:
Values:	

Community	Rating:
Values:	

Spirituality or religion	Rating:
Values:	

The next exercise helps you clarify and refine your values further by considering a wide range of possibilities (you can also download it at http://www.newharbinger.com/52311).

Common Values

Review this list and notice those that resonate with you most. Circle your top ten values, then from those ten, star the five that you care about most deeply.

Accountability	Citizenship	Creativity	Equality
Accuracy	Clear-mindedness	Curiosity	Excellence
Achievement	Collaboration	Decisiveness	Excitement
Adventure	Commitment	Dependability	Expertise
Altruism	Community	Determination	Exploration
Ambition	Compassion	Devoutness	Fairness
Assertiveness	Competency	Diligence	Faith
Authenticity	Competitiveness	Discipline	Family
Authority	Consistency	Discretion	Fitness
Balance	Contentment	Diversity	Fluency
Beauty	Continuous improvement	Economy	Focus
Belonging		Effectiveness	Freedom
Boldness	Contribution	Efficiency	Friendship
Calmness	Control	Elegance	Fun
Carefulness	Cooperation	Empathy	Generosity
Challenge	Correctness	Enjoyment	Grace
Cheerfulness	Courtesy	Enthusiasm	Gratitude

Growth	Legacy	Reliability	Strength
Hard work	Love	Resourcefulness	Structure
Health	Loyalty	Respectfulness	Success
Helping	Mastery	Responsibility	Support
Holiness	Merit	Restraint	Teamwork
Honesty	Obedience	Results-oriented	Temperance
Honor	Openness	Rigor	Thoroughness
Humility	Optimism	Security	Thoughtfulness
Independence	Order	Self-actualization	Timeliness
Influence	Originality	Self-control	Tolerance
Ingenuity	Patriotism	Self-reliance	Tradition
Inquisitiveness	Peace	Self-respect	Trustworthiness
Insightfulness	Piety	Selflessness	Truth-seeking
Intelligence	Poise	Sensitivity	Understanding
Intuition	Positivity	Serenity	Uniqueness
Joy	Practicality	Service	Unity
Justice	Preparedness	Simplicity	Usefulness
Kindness	Professionalism	Spirituality	Vision
Knowledge	Prudence	Spontaneity	Vitality
Leadership	Quality	Stability	Wisdom
Learning	Recognition	Stewardship	Worldliness

Daily Values-Based Action

Developing a daily values-based action practice will foster greater awareness of your values, help you increasingly honor them, and build confidence along the way. A routine practice will also help you remember to reflect on them during intense emotions and notice the difference between emotion-driven behaviors and values-based actions. Log your answers in a notes application on your cellphone or download several copies of each worksheet at http://www.newharbinger .com/52311—you can review these later to see your progress.

Daily Values Reflection

At the end of the day, reflect on a value you honored and notice how important that value is to you, rating it on a scale of 0 to 10, with 0 being not important at all and 10 being extremely important.

_____

_____

What specific actions did you take to honor that value, and what emotions did you have to accept to do so?

_____

_____

_____

What urges did you have to notice but disobey to honor that value?

_____

_____

_____

_____

The following worksheet will help you plan and reflect on your daily values-based actions (you can also download it at http://www.newharbinger.com/52311).

Daily Values-Based Actions Log

At the beginning of the day, choose a value you'd like to honor that day. Write out a specific values-based action you can realistically achieve given what's already on your plate. At the end of the day, reflect on whether you honored this value, and if not, identify the barriers that arose so you can navigate around them if they arise again. Notice and let go of any judgment or self-criticism that might arise; you are indeed taking new strides just in creating this daily practice. To help you remember this new practice, send yourself a text, set a reminder in your phone, or write the values-based action you'll take that day on a sticky note or index card.

Value: _____ Values-based action: _____

Taken Y/N: _____

Barriers if not taken and how to navigate them in the future: _____

_____

Value: _____ Values-based action: _____

Taken Y/N: _____

Barriers if not taken and how to navigate them in the future: _____

_____

Value: _____ Values-based action: _____

Taken Y/N: _____

Barriers if not taken and how to navigate them in the future: _____

_____

Value: _____ Values-based action: _____

Taken Y/N: _____

Barriers if not taken and how to navigate them in the future: _____

_____

Value: _____ Values-based action: _____

Taken Y/N: _____

Barriers if not taken and how to navigate them in the future: _____

_____

Value: _____ Values-based action: _____

Taken Y/N: _____

Barriers if not taken and how to navigate them in the future: _____

_____

Value: _____ Values-based action: _____

Taken Y/N: _____

Barriers if not taken and how to navigate them in the future: _____

_____

Summary

Values can help you do the things that are important to you even when that's difficult, and they are as individual as you are. With clarity on what your values are, you're empowered to choose either what your emotions dictate or what your values lead you to do. Your values are a guiding light to making decisions in the face of strong emotions and will support you in having emotionally intelligent interactions. Routinely practice reflecting on and honoring your values—this will help you notice, allow, and cope with your emotions in a healthy way.

CHAPTER 5

Emotion Coping

Negative emotions, as you know, trigger urges to take action or avoid. And these urges create moments of choice, where you can either engage in emotion-driven behaviors (that keep us stuck at the top of the wave) or act on your values. But some emotions are stronger and more triggering than others; some reach an intensity that sweeps away the ability to act on values. You're so swamped with pain that, depending on the emotion, you feel driven to attack, avoid, or withdraw.

When your attempts to ride the wave leave you overwhelmed and prey to emotion-driven behavior, you need additional resources. This chapter and the next will introduce you to emotion coping: six ways you can manage emotional pain so you can retain the choice to act on your values. In other words, emotion coping can help you turn down the knob of an emotion's intensity so that your life won't be dictated by action urges.

In this chapter, you'll learn three emotion coping processes:

- Mindfulness of the moment

- Relaxation

- Distraction

Mindfulness of the Moment: Five Senses

A quick way to achieve mindfulness of the moment is the five senses exercise. In this process you sequentially attend to each of your five senses, so you can observe what you're experiencing *right now*.

Five Senses Exercise

This 2.5-minute exercise shifts your attention from upsetting feelings and thoughts to physical experiences. But most important, it takes you out of your mind—where emotions are generated—and into the experience of the present moment.

- **Get into a comfortable position.**

- **What are you hearing?** For 30 seconds, observe all the sounds around you: verbal sounds (but don't get involved in tracking a conversation), sounds in your immediate environment, remote sounds. Everything from the ticking of a clock or the whoosh of the air conditioner to traffic or bird sounds.

- **What are you feeling?** For 30 seconds, notice sensations in your body; observe sensations as you sit or stand, while your body stays connected to the outside world. Notice temperature or texture where you're touching something.

- **What are you smelling?** For 30 seconds, observe any scent or odor in your environment. Do you have a scent—aftershave, cologne, shampoo? Can you detect a scent or odor from those around you? If you can't actually smell anything, notice the feeling of the air passing through your nose as you inhale—is it cool or warm? What does the breath feel like as it fills your lungs?

- **What do you see?** For 30 seconds, observe your visual environment. Notice shapes and contours; notice sizes and colors. Notice faces and expressions. Notice, if you can see it, the landscape and the sky.

- **What are you tasting?** For 30 seconds, observe any residual tastes in your mouth. There may be faint flavors from your last meal, or a sense of salt or sour. Pay attention to the sides of your tongue where your taste buds are located.

When using the five senses exercise for emotion coping, go through the cycle once, and then check (on a scale of 0 to 10) the intensity of the emotion. If it remains strong, and you don't yet feel able to act on your values, do another cycle with your five senses.

Relaxation

Relaxation processes can quickly impact and reduce the distress of negative emotions. Here you'll learn four of the most immediate and effective relaxation techniques available:

- Diaphragmatic breathing

- Body awareness and release

- Cue-controlled breathing

- Safe place visualization

Diaphragmatic Breathing

During an emotional upset, people often breathe in quick, shallow bursts. The diaphragm gets tight, and that constriction sends a message to the brain that something is wrong or threatening. Through diaphragmatic breathing, you can deliberately release stress and send a counter-message to your brain that all is well.

1. Find a place where you can practice quietly for 5 minutes. Sit up straight and put one hand on your abdomen (just above your belt line) and the other on your upper chest. As you inhale, draw the air downward, as if you were inflating your lower abdomen. Let your stomach expand slowly, hold the air for a moment, and then slowly exhale. During a diaphragmatic breath, the hand on your chest should hardly move, while the hand on your belly should gently press outward as you breathe in and slowly descend as you breathe out.

2. Now take a slow, deep breath in through your nose, letting it push out the hand on your abdomen. Then exhale slowly through your mouth, noticing how your hand moves inward again. Continue to breathe slowly, directing the air deeply into your abdomen, feeling your hand moving out and in with each breath.

3. Notice how each breath expands your stomach like a balloon. Also notice, as you breathe slowly and deeply, how your body begins to relax. Keep your attention on your breath, for ten breaths, counting each time you exhale. If your attention wanders and thoughts intrude, just bring your focus back to the breath—counting and watching the hand on your stomach move.

Practice diaphragmatic breathing for two rounds of ten breaths, at least once a day for the next week. If you have difficulty directing the breath into your abdomen, gently push your hand into your stomach as you exhale. Then, as you inhale, let the breath push back against the pressure of your hand.

In the next exercise, you will scan your entire body from feet to face while relaxing away tension in each major muscle group. It takes only 10 minutes, but the effect is often a significant reduction in stress and distress. You can follow along to a guided audio version of this visualization at http://www.newharbinger.com/52311 or make your own recording of this on your cellphone.

Body Awareness and Release

In a quiet place, sit or lie on your back.

Choose a cue word or phrase that you associate with relaxation, and that you'll recite internally as you release tension in each part of your body. The cue word could be a color or place that you find relaxing. It could be a relaxing word, such as "peace," "love," or "safe." It might just be encouragement such as "relax" when you breathe in and "let it go" as you breathe out.

With your cue word selected, take two diaphragmatic breaths, watching the hand on your abdomen press out and in with each breath.

[Pause]

Now bring your focus to your feet, becoming aware of any tension you feel there. Take a deep, diaphragmatic breath, saying your cue word at the top of the breath. Then exhale, releasing all tension in your feet with the out-breath.

[Pause]

Now notice any tension in your calves and shins. Take in a diaphragmatic breath, say your cue word, and exhale, releasing all tension in your calves and shins.

[Pause]

Notice any tension in your thighs and buttocks. Take in a diaphragmatic breath, saying your cue word at the top of the breath. Exhale, releasing all tension in your thighs and buttocks.

[Pause]

Now notice any tension in your stomach. Take a diaphragmatic breath and say your cue word at the top of the breath. As you exhale, relax away all tension in your stomach.

[Pause]

Observe any tension in your chest and back. Take a deep, diaphragmatic breath and say your cue word at the top. Relax away all tension in your chest and back as you exhale.

[Pause]

Now notice any tension in your arms. Take a diaphragmatic breath and say your cue word at the top of the breath. Now relax away any tension in your arms as you exhale.

[Pause]

At this moment, notice any tension in your neck and shoulders. Take a diaphragmatic breath and say your cue word at the top. Now relax away the tension in your neck and shoulders as you exhale.

[Pause]

Finally, notice any tension in your face and forehead. Take a diaphragmatic breath and say your cue word as you reach the top. As you release the breath, let go of any tension in your face and forehead.

[Pause]

Practice body awareness and release once a day for a week. If the exercise feels too long to you, try the short form: (1) feet, legs, and buttocks; (2) chest, abdomen, and back; (3) arms and shoulders; and (4) neck, face, and forehead.

Cue-Controlled Breathing

Cue-controlled breathing is a powerful relaxation technique that can soften distress and distressing emotions in a couple of minutes. It utilizes the cue word you've already learned to use but applies cue- and breath-based relaxation to your entire body at once, rather than smaller muscle groups. You can use cue-controlled breathing anywhere, anytime—it's instantly available when you need it.

1. Start with diaphragmatic breathing.

2. Then just for a few seconds, scan your entire body for tension and stress.

3. As you continue diaphragmatic breathing, say your cue word to yourself with each inhale.

4. As you exhale, allow your whole body to relax. Release all tension, everywhere inside, as you let go of the breath.

5. Repeat until your emotional distress has noticeably subsided—usually three to ten breaths.

Because cue-controlled breathing is a brief process, you're encouraged to practice at least two or three times a day for a week or two. That should be enough for you to use it effectively when you're beset by strong emotions.

Another method to help manage intense emotions is visualizing a place that evokes peace and helps calm the body's fight-flight-or-freeze response. Your body and mind will react with nearly the same intensity to an imagined versus a real situation. Whatever you focus on, actual or merely visualized, will impact you emotionally and physically. A safe place visualization uses this fact to create a sense of peace and calm—even when you're caught in emotional distress. You can follow along to a guided audio version of this visualization at http://www.newharbinger.com/52311 or make a recording of this on your cellphone and find a quiet place to listen.

Safe Place Visualization

Select a place where you've felt safe and happy, where you were immune to hurt or injury. It could be your childhood bedroom, a beautiful place where you experienced calm and content, or a place to which you've traveled or where you lived. It could even be pure fantasy or a place described in a favorite piece of fiction. It doesn't matter as long as imagining this place triggers a feeling of peace and safety.

Close your eyes and take two diaphragmatic breaths. Now imagine you're entering your safe place. Notice everything you can see—the shapes and colors. Pay attention to the details—are you inside or outside, can you see the sky and horizon or the furniture in a room? Are there certain trusted people there? Are there animals? Make sure there are locks, walls, or security if you need it.

What sounds do you hear, both close and far away? Try to notice every possible sound that goes with the safe place. Can you hear wind, waves, a conversation? Make sure there is something soothing to hear.

Is there a singular smell in your safe place, such as flowers, the ocean, or grass? For a moment, see if you can enjoy any fragrance that's part of this special environment.

What physical feelings do you have in this place? Do you feel the weight of a blanket or beach sand? Do you feel warm or cool? What are you touching—notice the texture and feel. Is air moving through a window or from a breeze outside?

Now hold it all together as you continue to enjoy this safe place. Notice everything you see, hear, smell, and feel. Let it relax you and soften any emotional distress. You are safe here, free from hurt and harm, wrapped in beauty and comfort.

This is your private place. It's for no one but you. The peace and contentment are yours alone. You can return to this safe place anytime you want. As soon as you start the visualization, you will be there.

Look around once more; hold in your mind each detail. Now, as you did in the beginning, take two more diaphragmatic breaths. Open your eyes and return to your surroundings—taking the feeling of peace and safety with you.

Practice safe place visualization once a day for a week so that the images come easily and you can hold them in the face of an upsetting emotion. After a few times through this exercise you may find you don't need the recording anymore—the image will show up as soon as you call it to mind.

Daily Relaxation Practice

You are encouraged to practice each of the relaxation exercises described above at least seven times, and more in the case of cue-controlled breathing. This is important. These skills need to be well learned and easily accessible so that they'll help reduce your distress in the presence of strong emotions. To keep on track with your practice, use the following log to record your experiences (you can also download it at http://www.newharbinger.com/52311).

Relaxation Practice Log

Put a check mark for each technique practiced on a given day. Put two check marks if a technique is practiced twice in a day.

Technique	Day 1	Day 2	Day 3	Day 4	Day 5	Day 6	Day 7
Diaphragmatic Breathing							
Body Awareness and Release							
Cue-Controlled Breathing							
Safe Place Visualization							

Distraction

In the face of strong emotional pain, distraction has been proven to be a good coping strategy. That's because it redirects your attention to something other than your distress. Distraction is well worth learning to get temporary emotional relief. However, distraction used excessively, with the aim to avoid emotions altogether, is problematic. Chronic emotional suppression—through distraction or any other means—has the paradoxical effect of making emotions *more* intense over time, limiting your emotion efficacy and eroding your confidence in emotion acceptance. It gets you stuck at the top of the wave. The key is to use distraction skills to help you then access your emotion acceptance and emotion coping skills. Once distraction has reduced the emotional intensity, ride the emotion wave.

Brief distraction—just long enough for your distress to soften—can be achieved in multiple ways without facilitating problematic avoidance:

- *Focus on pleasant events in the past or future:* Think of beautiful places you've been, happy experiences, memories of success, or moments of achievement; plan a vacation, special event, or project; daydream about meeting someone special.

- *Focus on someone else:* Think of ways you could be of service to others, connect with a friend, call someone in your family, watch people as they go by, think of someone you care about and what they might be doing right now, or imagine having a fun, lively conversation with a friend and what they might say that would make you feel better.

- *Focus on something else:* Pay attention to any nearby natural beauty, walk around your neighborhood or a park and notice the scenery, watch a video, read a book or magazine, play an instrument, write in your journal, go online to learn something, or listen to music, a podcast, or an audiobook.

- *Be productive:* Do some necessary chore or task, clean a room in your home, organize something, make necessary appointments, work in your garden, do your homework, exercise, or pay bills.

- *Do something pleasurable:* Eat something you enjoy, sew, knit or crochet, go on a day trip to a favorite spot, watch sports, go shopping, draw, paint, write, do something creative, enjoy sexual thoughts and fantasies, pray or meditate, play an online game, check in with social media, take a nap, do a physical activity you enjoy (biking, swimming, hiking, shooting baskets, or yoga), or work on a hobby.

- *Leave where you are:* Stop what you're doing and go somewhere else; try something simple, like taking a walk (smell the air, observe, listen to what's around you); or go outside or into a different room.

- *Count:* Count each out-breath up to ten and then start over, every red car you see on the street, the number of a certain type of car, the number of trees on a block, the number of green or yellow objects in your house, how many states you've visited, the good movies you've seen this year. To some people, counting might seem to be a useless activity, but it can provide brief yet real relief when emotions threaten to overwhelm you.

Practice Emotion Coping

It's time to build your emotion coping skills in the face of distressing feelings. To practice coping, you'll start with something you already know how to do—emotion surfing. Here's the process:

1. Choose a recent situation that can still trigger an emotional reaction.

2. Visualize everything you can see in the scene. Pay attention to what you hear—voices or ambient sounds in the environment. Notice your sense of touch—temperature and texture, as well as what your body feels like.

3. Watch for an emotional reaction. When your distress reaches 5 to 6 (on a scale of 0 to 10), shut off the scene and start emotion surfing (from chapter 3): Observe your body's sensations, feelings (rating distress from 0 to 10), thoughts (always letting them go), and action urges. See where you are on the wave. Try as much as you can to accept the emotion and its elements. Keep surfing for 2 to 3 minutes.

4. Now stop surfing and shift to the emotion coping strategy you want to practice—the five senses, relaxation, or some form of distraction. Again, notice the emotion's intensity (0 to 10). Practice your coping strategy for 2 to 5 minutes. Keep checking for emotional intensity every 30 seconds or so. As soon as the emotional pain begins to noticeably reduce, you're finished with the exercise.

You're encouraged to practice emotion coping, at least once, with:

*   Five senses exercise

*   Diaphragmatic breathing

*   Cue-controlled breathing

*   Safe place visualization

- One or two distraction techniques that appeal to you

Experiment to find out which of these emotion coping skills works best. Then use them when an emotion is so intense that you can't access your emotion surfing or relaxation skills. Be careful not to rely on just one skill. Find several that work for you. During an upset, if one skill fails to calm you, you can shift to another in your repertoire of coping strategies. And remember, if you can act on your values when triggered, do it. If you can't, cope.

Let's see how this works in real life. Here's an example of Enrique emotion surfing.

Enrique has struggled with sadness and anger. Situations where he's experienced some disappointment seem to be most triggering. There have been so many:

- *When his partner doesn't seem interested in shared activities*

- *When something he wants to buy isn't available*

- *When his foot acts up and he can't play tennis*

- *When his daughter gets a poor grade in school*

- *When he is assigned a task at work he doesn't like*

As Enrique surfs, he notices that the first emotion is sadness—something he wanted, perhaps counted on, isn't happening. Then anger starts to blend in along with blaming thoughts.

Enrique has been working on allowing and accepting the disappointment while he surfs. He has also been practicing acting on his core values of kindness and caring despite urges to say mean things or act disgusted.

Sometimes Enrique can find a way to be kind, but there are moments when his emotions overwhelm him and he goes on the attack. This is particularly concerning in triggering situations with his partner, daughter, and boss.

Enrique chooses his coping strategies. The five senses exercise didn't work for him because he's annoyed that he can't seem to smell or taste anything. But diaphragmatic breathing (combined with cue-controlled breathing) has worked well for him. He's also found the safe place visualization to be relaxing. For distraction, he chose reading (mystery novels) and walking in a park near his house. He also likes light weight lifting.

Enrique identified a half dozen fairly recent situations where his disappointment/anger has been triggered. He begins by imagining one of those scenes—what he can see, hear, and touch—until he can feel the disappointment. At around midway in the distress scale, he cuts off the scene and emotion surfs. It doesn't take long for anger to start weaving into the sadness. He watches the sensations in his body, his thoughts, and his action urge to say something attacking. Then he notices where he is on the wave.

Enrique watches for another cycle (sensations, feelings, thoughts, urges), trying to accept what he experiences. Then he shifts to coping. He rates the strength of his feeling (0 to 10) and begins to do cue-controlled breathing—taking slow diaphragmatic in-breaths, saying his cue word, and relaxing away tension throughout his body on the out-breath.

Every 30 seconds or so, he checks to see where he is on the distress scale. After three minutes of cue-controlled breathing, Enrique is down from 5 to 2.

Enrique repeats surfing plus coping. For each selected coping strategy, he goes through the procedure. During each practice session, after several minutes of emotion surfing, he checks his distress level and starts emotion coping. Once he stops surfing, it takes an average of 3 to 5 minutes to see a significant reduction in distress.

In the end, Enrique chooses cue-controlled breathing, reading, and weight lifting (if he's at home) to cope with high-intensity feelings.

To use emotion coping in real life, Enrique began using his three preferred techniques when he noticed a wave of disappointment that overwhelmed his commitment to kindness and caring. The greatest challenge was remembering and taking the time to do his breathing. When he remembered, the emotion coping always seemed to help.

Using Emotion Coping When Triggered

This is the point where all your practice helps you begin coping in real life. Start by being clear about your preferred coping strategies—which ones you like and work best for you. Now, whenever you get emotionally triggered, surf and observe the emotion. Notice the moment of choice. Remember the values-based behavior you want to use. If the emotion overwhelms the commitment to your values, start emotion coping. Keep at it until the distress level drops. If one coping strategy isn't helping, switch to another. Continue coping until you feel ready to act on your values.

Summary

Learning how to quickly and effectively turn down difficult emotional responses is an empowering life skill. It can build confidence in emotion management and allow you to then see the values-based choices available to you. You're on the verge of big changes in your life. Emotion surfing plus coping can give you the resources you need to face any feeling, even the most overwhelming ones, and still honor your values.

CHAPTER 6

Managing Overwhelming Emotions

In chapter 5, you learned several critical coping skills to use when emotions feel overwhelming, when action urges threaten to push you into emotion-driven behavior (avoid, attack, withdraw), and when you begin to feel stuck at the top of the wave. While often highly effective, these coping strategies may take a few minutes to initiate. In this chapter, you'll learn emotion coping in the moment: evidence-based techniques you can use in 30 to 60 seconds or less.

These coping skills aren't designed to avoid emotions; that will, unfortunately, cause more distress in the long run. As with the skills in chapter 5, emotion coping in the moment should be used when an upset overwhelms your ability to act on your values, and when surfing and observing an emotion aren't enough. The resources you'll learn now will strengthen your emotion efficacy, offering new choices you can use *immediately* no matter how overwhelmed or prone to emotionally reactive behavior you might feel.

In this chapter you'll learn three emotion coping in the moment processes:

- Self-soothing

- Coping thoughts

- Radical acceptance

Self-Soothing

All five of your senses—touch, sight, smell, taste, hearing—can register distress. And all five senses can soothe and quiet your distress. Self-soothing is the deliberate harnessing of each sense modality to create feelings of calm, even peace.

What follows is a list of self-soothing activities, organized by sensory experience. Look over the list and mark the box for activities likely to soothe you. Next, you can experiment with each selected activity to learn which ones work best for you. Everyone is unique and will gravitate to different soothing experiences. Some, for example, find ocean sounds relaxing, while others feel an undernote of anxiety while listening to the power of the sea. Some relax with the smell of flowers, while others find floral scents cloying, or even a reminder of funerals. So choose only self-soothing activities that you're drawn to and willing to try.

When you begin experimenting, observe your reaction to each activity. If it doesn't begin to relax you in 30 to 60 seconds, try it in combination with diaphragmatic breathing. Should that produce no result, drop it. Once you've discovered four to six self-soothing practices that *seem* to work, it will be time to try them during an actual emotion exposure.

Soothing with Touch

- ☐ Wrap yourself in a warm, heavy blanket.

- ☐ Massage your temples, neck, or shoulders.

- ☐ Carry and touch a small object that connects you to someone you love.

- ☐ Carry and touch a smooth, soft, or velvety piece of cloth.

- ☐ Carry and touch a smooth, water-polished stone.

- ☐ Touch and look at a piece of jewelry that represents beauty, peace, and calmness.

- ☐ Carry and touch worry beads, a rosary, a Jewish star, a cross, or other objects that connect you to a spiritual core.

- ☐ Caress one hand with the other.

- ☐ Take a hot bath or shower.

- ☐ Close your eyes and vigorously rub the palms of your hands together until they're warm. Gently place them over your eyelids.

Soothing with Sight

☐ Carry soothing pictures in your purse, wallet, or on your phone.

☐ Carry a photo of someone you love and who makes you want to be your best self.

☐ Carry photos of a place you love and where you have been happy.

☐ Carry or have on your phone a mandala or an image on which to focus and meditate.

☐ Look around you to find the most beautiful thing in your environment. Give it your full attention.

☐ Look around you to find something that sparks your interest and curiosity.

☐ Look for objects around you that have your favorite (or most peaceful) color.

Soothing with Smell

☐ Carry a vial or an object that has your favorite fragrance, or a fragrance used by someone you love.

☐ Burn a scented candle or incense.

☐ Go into your kitchen and smell vanilla, chocolate, or some savory scent that reminds you of delicious and comforting food.

☐ Wash your hands in a fragrant soap and massage your jaw and forehead with them.

☐ If you are outside, enjoy the outdoor smells of earth and flowers, trees and grass, or open your window and inhale.

☐ Rub your hands together vigorously and then smell them. This is you, your precious self—a reminder to treat yourself kindly.

☐ Apply your favorite scented lotion.

Soothing with Taste

☐ Suck on a mint or chew your favorite gum.

☐ Carry a favorite food with you to snack on when you're upset.

☐ Make or carry a thermos of your favorite hot beverage. Drink it slowly, savoring every sip.

☐ Eat a juicy piece of fruit very slowly. If away from home, carry dried fruit, such as raisins. Chew slowly to unlock the flavor.

☐ Carry and eat cashews, almonds, or other favorite nuts.

☐ Sip cold water, feeling the cool, quenching, calming liquid in your mouth.

Soothing with Hearing

☐ Create a library of soothing music, accessible on your cellphone. Select calming pieces when you're upset.

☐ Listen to audiobooks or engaging podcasts.

☐ Listen to a calming meditation.

☐ Listen to a file of soothing nature or water sounds (rain, waves, babbling brook, etc.).

☐ Open your window and listen to birds or wind sounds, even distant traffic and city sounds if you find them relaxing.

☐ Turn on your personal water fountain.

☐ Listen to a recording of a calming mantra.

☐ Listen to videos online of cats purring.

☐ Listen to ASMR (autonomous sensory meridian response) videos online.

Experimenting

Once you've marked a group of self-soothing activities that have the potential to relax and calm you, it's time to experiment. Set aside a half hour or so to test them. Try each one for a few minutes and observe the effect. Is it relaxing, neutral, or even annoying? If your response is neutral—you can detect no impact—try the soothing activity in combination with diaphragmatic breathing to see whether there's a synergistic effect. If you notice feeling annoyed, move on to another activity.

Now, after experimenting, you'll have a list of soothing experiences that may help you regulate intense emotions. You're ready to test them with real, distressing feelings (see Practice Emotion Coping in chapter 5).

Coping Thoughts

In the same way that self-instruction can help you learn a new task (for example, knitting a sweater or wiring your home entertainment center), research has shown that coping thoughts can be a way to encourage and coach yourself through intense emotional waves. They are a reminder of your strength and the ability to survive distressing experiences.

The following coping thoughts are examples of how real individuals have navigated the white water rapids of emotional pain (adapted from McKay, Davis, and Fanning 2021). Put a check mark next to the five or more best coping thoughts that might work for you. Later you can test their effectiveness during emotion exposures.

- ☐ Don't fight it; just allow it and it will pass.

- ☐ Let thoughts go; just ride the wave.

- ☐ Accept, don't fight your emotions.

- ☐ Accept, do not listen in (to thoughts).

- ☐ This, too, shall pass; emotions don't last forever.

☐ I've been through other painful experiences, and I survived.

☐ My feelings are hard to have, but I can accept them.

☐ I can be anxious and still deal with the situation.

☐ I can be sad and still do what I need to do.

☐ I'm strong enough to handle what's happening to me right now.

☐ This is an opportunity for me to learn how to cope with my emotions.

☐ I can navigate through this; I have before.

☐ I can ride this wave and not get overwhelmed.

☐ I can take all the time I need to have this feeling and watch it slowly recede.

☐ I've survived other situations like this before, and I can survive this one.

☐ My anger/fear/sadness won't kill me; it's just hard right now.

☐ These are just my feelings; they are temporary.

☐ It's okay to feel sad/angry/afraid sometimes.

☐ My feelings and thoughts don't control my life; I do.

☐ I'm not in danger right now.

☐ It's just pain—I can handle it.

☐ The situation sucks, but it's only temporary.

☐ I'm strong and I can deal with this.

☐ Accept, accept, accept.

These examples might also give you ideas for coping thoughts of your own. See if you can combine or modify some of them, or generate original coping thoughts tailored for feelings and situations you often face. Use the following worksheet to record the coping thoughts that will work for you (you can also download it at http://www.newharbinger.com/52311).

My Coping Thoughts

In the space below, write each coping thought you marked as well as new ones you created.

The previous list of coping thoughts was for general use. Now you'll use the following worksheet to apply your list of coping thoughts to specific situations. A sample worksheet is included first, and then you can use the blank one to write your own responses (you can also download it at http://www.newharbinger.com/52311).

Situation-Specific Coping Thoughts

On the following worksheet, in the column labeled "Distressing Situation," list up to ten events that can trigger distressing emotions. In the "New Coping Thoughts" column, choose and write down the most appropriate coping thought from your list above. If seeing an example would be helpful, you can check out Leticia's coping thoughts below.

Coping Thoughts Worksheet

Distressing Situation	New Coping Thought

Here's how Leticia completed her Coping Thoughts Worksheet.

Coping Thoughts Worksheet Example: Leticia

Distressing Situation	New Coping Thought
1. Feeling overwhelmed. Missing friends at my old job.	1. It's a wave; don't fight it, and it will pass.
2. Morning sadness; don't feel like getting up.	2. I can be sad and still do what I need to do.
3. My mother calls. Sick with chemo side effects. So afraid for her and me.	3. I'm strong enough to face this. I won't run away.
4. My partner complains that I'm "disengaged." Feel hurt and angry.	4. Hurt and anger won't kill me; it's just hard right now.
5. Anxious I'll fail at my new job.	5. It's okay to be anxious; I can ride the wave and it will pass.
6. Feeling lonely, disconnected from partner.	6. This feeling comes and goes. I need to get busy and stay focused.
7. Wrist hurts; flare-up of carpal tunnel. Anxious.	7. I've dealt with this before, and I can overcome it again.
8. Sunday night anxiety about difficult week ahead. Want to give up, go to bed.	8. These are just feelings that will change. I can do something productive.
9. Home alone with my thoughts. Anxious and sad.	9. My thoughts don't control me; I can go enjoy some nature.
10. Missed deadline. Boss complains; anxious.	10. Ride the wave; it'll pass. I've solved problems like this before.

Radical Acceptance

Nonacceptance of an emotion, or the events and choices that led to it, is a direct route to sustained emotional pain. It will keep you stuck at the top of the wave. As soon as you judge yourself for having a particular feeling, as soon as you tell yourself, "I shouldn't feel *x*," the lock springs closed and you get caught in your distress. The same is true for nonacceptance of the circumstances that trigger a painful emotion. Blaming yourself or someone else, raging that it should never have happened, only compounds your pain. Now you're sad or scared *and* angry. *And* roiling in self-blame.

You can't change what's occurred—whatever you or others did. Nonacceptance, claiming it shouldn't have happened, is a form of "undoing." But it doesn't work. The events and choices did happen, and your emotional wave must run its course. Accepting the wave *and* the circumstances is the only way not to get caught in chronic emotional pain.

Radical acceptance doesn't mean you condone or agree with what happened. It just means you've stopped fighting it. It doesn't mean you like what you feel, just that you're willing to feel it. Here are some suggested acceptance thoughts to help you face difficult events and allow painful feelings. Check the ones that appeal to you.

- ☐ This is the way it has to be.

- ☐ I feel *x*; I can have this feeling.

- ☐ All the events have led up to now.

- ☐ I can't change what's already happened.

- ☐ This is what happened; my feelings are valid.

- ☐ It's no use fighting the past.

- ☐ How I feel is how I feel—no use judging it.

- ☐ Fighting the past only blinds me to what I need to do now.

☐ It's a waste of time to fight what's already happened.

☐ I'll make room for what I feel.

☐ Accept, accept, accept.

☐ This moment is a result of a million other decisions.

☐ I accept what I did and how I feel; I'll go on from here.

☐ This moment is exactly as it should be, given what happened before it.

☐ Even if I don't like it, the present is exactly what it needs to be.

Radical acceptance builds a new relationship to the present moment. There are no longer "shoulds" about what's happened and how you feel—you are just making room for it. Allowing it. Permitting what is—even if painful—to just be. This is how we get better, how we heal: by allowing this moment, and the ones before, to just be.

Now, as you did in chapter 5, it's time to practice. The best way to learn emotion coping in the moment is by exposing yourself to emotions triggered by a recent upsetting event (emotion surfing). Before starting the next exercise, choose which coping processes you want to experiment with to see whether they reduce emotional pain. Include:

• At least three self-soothing strategies

• At least three coping thoughts

• Two or three acceptance thoughts

During exposures, you can combine or use a single coping process. You can follow along to a guided audio version of this visualization at http://www.newharbinger.com/52311 or make a recording of this on your cellphone.

Exposure-Based Emotion Coping

Choose a recent situation that can stir you emotionally. Make sure it's something you can call to mind with relative ease. As you practice exposures, you'll probably need to identify more than one triggering event. They tend to lose their emotional intensity with repeated visualizations.

Visualize everything you can see in the scene. Also notice what you hear—voices, conversation, or ambient sounds in the environment. Pay attention to your sense of touch—the temperature and texture of your surroundings. What does your body feel like? Hot, tight, sinking?

While continuing to observe the scene, watch for the start of an emotional reaction. How strong is it (on a scale of 0 to 10)? Keep watching and rating your emotion until it reaches 5 to 6 on the scale. Now shut off the scene; stop all attempts to visualize what happened.

Start emotion surfing. Notice your body sensations, feelings (always rating distress from 0 to 10), thoughts (always letting them go as soon as you recognize them), and action urges. Allow them to be as they are.

See where you are on the wave from 0 to 10. Keep surfing for 2 to 3 minutes.

Now it's time to practice emotion coping in the moment. Stop surfing and focus on one or a combination of:

Self-soothing activities

Coping thoughts

Accepting thoughts

Cue-controlled or diaphragmatic breathing

Practice your emotion coping skills for a few minutes, or until your distress rating is at a 4 or below or you're able to fully accept your distress without judgment, self-criticism, or giving into the emotion urges.

Keep experimenting with exposures until you've determined the effectiveness of each selected or combined coping strategy. Do further practice with the ones that seem to work. You can only really learn them when practicing in an upset state—because that's exactly the condition when you'll need them.

When it comes to real-time emotional upsets, you shouldn't rely on just one coping skill. You will often need multiple coping strategies, used sequentially and repeatedly, to manage an upset. And you may need more than a few minutes of coping to bring your distress level down.

When facing real-time distress, the first question is, how much time do you have? If there's little time to manage your feelings, use a breath-based coping strategy (from chapter 5) or self-soothing, coping thoughts, or acceptance thoughts from this chapter. Keep coping with several strategies, repeating as needed, until your distress diminishes.

If you have more time or space to cope with an upset, you'll have the opportunity to use more elaborate coping procedures, such as the five senses exercise, body awareness and release, and safe place visualization from chapter 5. Whichever coping process you choose, or have time for, keep coping until you feel better and the distress has fallen to a level where you feel able to act on your values (see chapter 4).

Let's see how this works in real life. Here's an example of Ricky practicing emotion coping.

Ricky is a nonbinary senior in high school and uses they/them pronouns. They often feel strongly reactive—mostly with feelings of anxiety (fear of rejection) and shame. People seem to ignore them or say critical or judgmental things. Ricky is most triggered when people:

- *Look away or roll their eyes*

- *Shrug and create physical distance when Ricky joins a group*

- *Engage in sotto voce ridicule actually intended for Ricky to hear: "Oh no, here they come." "Did Grandma buy that sweater?"*

- *Say critical things and don't invite Ricky to hang out*

Ricky's usual reaction is burning shame and withdrawal, followed by anxiety about how they might be rejected next time. Ricky used the above events and others for emotion exposure. They imagined the scene, trying to see, hear, and feel everything connected to the event. They kept "watching" until the shame and/or anxiety mounted to a 5 or 6. The goal was to surf the emotions, trying to accept the feelings and thoughts without judgment.

If Ricky were facing these emotions in real time, they would try to act on their core values of independence, self-respect, and honesty. But now, during exposure practice, Ricky shuts off the scene as soon as emotions reach midrange and starts using their preselected coping strategies:

- *Carrying and touching a green serpentine stone (given by their much-loved grandmother) while taking slow, deep breaths.*

- *Listening to waterfall sounds while taking deep breaths.*

- *Coping thought: "Some people love me; I love me."*

- *Coping thought: "I've been through this a million times—just ride the wave."*

- *Coping thought: "It's their problem, not mine. Accept, don't listen in to thoughts."*

- *Coping thought: "I'm strong enough to handle this; feelings pass."*

- *Acceptance thought: "That's the way they are; this is how they act."*

- *Acceptance thought: "I'm a target because I'm different."*

- *Acceptance thought: "I'm afraid of being hurt. I accept that. But I'm strong enough to face them and deal."*

Once Ricky shuts off the scene, they begin coping. In this particular exposure, they are practicing:

- *Touching the serpentine stone while doing diaphragmatic breathing.*

- *Adding the coping thought: "People love me; I love me." "I've been through this a million times—just ride the wave."*

- *Adding the acceptance thought: "This stuff happens; that's the way they are. I'm strong enough to face them and deal."*

Ricky coped for an average of 3 to 4 minutes during each exposure. They rubbed the stone and continued deep breathing the whole time, while repeating coping and acceptance thoughts—almost like a mantra. Distress typically dropped from 7 to 3 while Ricky coped. Some coping and acceptance thoughts worked better than others; they dropped the ones that were least effective.

Ricky also mixed in coping skills from chapter 5, particularly body awareness and release and safe place visualization. Over the course of multiple weeks of practice, Ricky became increasingly confident in their emotion coping skills. They were ready for real-time, real-life coping, which they practiced next.

At school, the looks, slights, and mumbled comments keep happening. In the aftermath of each occurrence, Ricky surfs the wave. They watch the swell and ebb of shame and anxiety. There are times when Ricky can act on their values of honesty and self-respect, asking "What are you saying? Be honest." They disarm their bullies with quips like, "Thanks, I'm glad you like my sweater too." But there are times when the pain just feels overwhelming. Then Ricky copes it down to a level where they can shrug off the hurt or confront the offending person.

Just as with Ricky, there will be a day when you're ready to use coping in the moment in real time. You will have identified and practiced your preferred coping strategies, while discarding the ones that don't work.

Now, when you get triggered, your first reaction can be to observe—just watching and surfing the wave. In some cases, observing and surfing will be enough, and you can move directly to acting on your values. But sometimes the pain will surge and overwhelm you. When that happens, values-based choices go out the window. It's time to employ all your best emotion coping skills— breathing techniques, relaxation skills, distracting and soothing yourself, and using coping and acceptance thoughts. Keep going until the pain diminishes. If one strategy doesn't work, switch to another until you feel able to respond to the situation effectively.

Summary

The processes we've discussed result in emotion efficacy. This is not a distant, ephemeral goal. Emotion efficacy can become a part of your life *right now*. Each time you practice emotion surfing and emotion coping, you clear the path to using it during difficult conversations, the subject of the next chapter.

CHAPTER 7

Communicating Skillfully

Having difficult conversations is inevitable. Two people cannot always have the same needs, desires, opinions, and abilities. Maybe you want to implement a boundary in a relationship, resign from your job, or advocate for yourself or others. While emotionally evocative topics and conflicting perspectives may be uncomfortable, resolution can ironically build trust, connection, and safety, strengthening the relationship. The capacity to express your perspective is supported by your ability to be aware of and skillfully manage your emotions, notice others' feelings, and use that information to communicate clearly.

Knowing your emotions and being able to self-reflect on an unmet need will help you determine *what* to communicate to others, and assertive communication is *how* to express those needs skillfully. In doing the exercises in this chapter, you might be surprised to discover that most people appreciate assertiveness—it helps them hear your perspective, interests, and needs without doing guesswork. The emotion surfing skills you've learned in the preceding chapters will further support you in identifying unmet needs and managing emotions that show up as you express yourself effectively.

The next three chapters will teach you science-backed, tried-and-true ways to express yourself while building connection with others. This chapter teaches a gradual approach to increasingly using assertive communication to express yourself clearly and respectfully make requests. Chapter 8 will guide you in how to deepen connection through attunement, a series of skills used to reassure others we hear them and are tuned in to what they're communicating. Chapter 9 offers practices to express empathy to others, helping strengthen relationships and rebuild them after disconnection. The skills in these chapters build off each other, easing the path to the next set of skills. Once you've finished the exercises in chapters 7, 8, and 9, then you're ready to put it all together in chapter 10.

Bringing Discomfort with You

Anticipating or experiencing conflict can trigger your nervous system's fight-flight-or-freeze response. This activation is a natural reaction to what your mind and body perceive as threatening or dangerous in some way, even if in reality that might not be the case. If past experiences of conflict left you feeling humiliated, punished, demoralized, intimidated, hurt, or angry, your mind and body may try to protect you by sending you signals to be on alert. Knowing this and managing the emotions that arise can help you get regrounded when this occurs. Such painful memories of past conflict and the expectations born out of them can shape your behavior in the face of discord now. The following worksheet will help you gain clarity on those painful experiences so that you can make space for the difficult emotions that may arise and manage conflict skillfully. You can also download the worksheet at http://www.newharbinger.com/52311.

===== My Relationship to Conflict =====

To help you embrace the discomfort that might arise when you anticipate or are experiencing tension, conflict, or a disagreement with someone, let's reflect on similar experiences from your past.

In the face of difficult conversations or conflict, I tend to experience the following:

Emotions: _____

_____

Physical sensations: _____

_____

Thoughts: _____

_____

_____

Urges: _____

_____

_____

What expectations do you have about others during conflict or disagreements based on your past experiences? Be specific (e.g., I expect people to yell at me, dismiss my feelings, refuse to take accountability, steamroll me, or shut down or withdraw).

_____

_____

_____

How confident are you in your ability to resolve conflict so that each party feels heard and respected and a resolution or compromise is achieved? Rate it on a scale of 0 to 10, with 0 being no confidence and 10 being the most confident. _____

Reconnecting with your values, what makes resolving conflict or arriving at a compromise important to you? Feel free to return to chapter 4 for a refresher on your values.

_____

_____

_____

_____

You've just laid some important groundwork to ease the process of effectively communicating in the face of challenges. When we expect that a difficult conversation or addressing conflict will be overwhelming, painful, or unproductive, we're more prone to approach it with skepticism and fear. When we expect a positive outcome from a challenging interaction or working through conflict, we can approach it with an open mind and see it as an opportunity to improve the relationship. Your work is to notice your expectations and hold them lightly, while making room for the full emotions that arise. Because your emotions will show up uninvited anyway, there's no need to avoid discomfort or try to push it away. Instead, allow the experience to be exactly as it is and use your emotion surfing skills to support you in communicating with clarity.

Communication Styles

Effective communication entails a combination of verbal and nonverbal skills that are tailored to the person to whom you're speaking, as well as the topic and context of the interaction (e.g., the environment, type of relationship, roles, "emotional baggage" between parties, past unresolved conflict). Communicating skillfully requires the following:

- Recognizing and managing strong emotions

- Being present with your emotions as well as others'

- Being willing to trust yourself

- Asserting your needs and making requests to meet them

- Being able to listen attentively and remain open-minded

- Responding to and expressing what matters most while avoiding punishing behaviors

- Believing that resolution is in both parties' interests

- Being aware of and respecting differences with others

With those tenets of healthy and effective communication in mind, we'll look at four common styles of communication. Knowing your typical style or the style you tend to default to during challenging interactions can build more awareness of this pattern and help you notice opportunities to pivot to a healthy communication style. How we each adopt our predominant communication style or styles is a chapter (or even a book) unto itself. Some of the most common ways problematic communication styles become programmed are as a means of coping with an aggressor or in the face of trauma, from observational learning (adopting another's approach), as a result of punishment from others when healthy communication is used, or as a by-product of chronic low self-esteem. As you read through the styles and see what resonates, practice self-kindness by letting go of any self-criticism or judgment that may arise. We don't get to choose our upbringing nor all of our role models in life (positive or negative), but we do get to choose how to kindly make space for that context and practice a healthy approach.

Passive Communication

Passive communication occurs when you avoid expressing your opinions, emotions, perspectives, or needs and prioritize those of others. As unmet needs mount due to not being expressed, they build into resentment and annoyance and reach a point at which expressing them can no longer be avoided. This can result in emotional hijacking and angry outbursts. Because explosive outbursts are unusual for this type of communicator, feeling shame, guilt, and remorse for expressing intense emotions can arise and prompt a quick retreat back to a passive communication style. Passive communication can take many forms and may look like:

- Self-sacrificing by putting others' needs repeatedly over your own

- Failing to assert yourself or self-advocate

- Allowing others to make choices for you

- Keeping your emotions, needs, perspectives, or opinions to yourself

- Avoiding eye contact during tension, disagreements, or conflict

- Speaking with a soft or quiet tone of voice

- Communicating apologetically or without confidence

- Slumping down or making yourself small

Passive communicators use this approach to avoid the likelihood of conflict, judgment from others, or the emotional discomfort they perceive may come from self-expression. Consequently, they often feel stuck, helpless, anxious, or resentful for not expressing themselves. They may also feel confused and have difficulty knowing what they stand for after repeatedly ignoring their own feelings or needs. Furthermore, emotional maturity can become stymied from the recurrent absence of addressing needs and resolving disagreements.

Aggressive Communication

Aggressive communicators tend to express themselves and their emotions strongly without considering others' needs, desires, or feelings. They express themselves in a dominating and uncompromising style that can feel disrespectful, condescending, or abusive to others. This way of communicating is often accompanied by interrupting others, not listening fully, defensiveness, and expressing frustration. Over time, aggressive communicators may feel estranged from others, have few close relationships, frequently experience short-lived relationships, and feel misunderstood or disliked by others. Aggressive communication can look like:

- Quickly expressing impatience, irritability, and frustration

- Speaking in a loud tone of voice

- Using intimidating body postures, such as standing close to others or pointing

- Frequently interrupting

- Being unwilling or unable to consider the other person's experience

- Expressing anger or defensiveness with little provocation

- Humiliating, blaming, or harshly criticizing others

- Expressing disappointment that others have not met unrealistically high standards

- Being unwilling to compromise and/or insisting that only you are "right"

Aggressive communicators often use this approach to maintain feeling in control and avoid feeling insecure or anxious. This pattern of exerting an unreasonable amount of influence and control over others' lives can create a false sense of confidence, but it results in relationships that are strained, tense, and lack closeness, as others are afraid to interact with or open up to them. Often, aggressive communicators have unsatisfying relationships and feel isolated and misunderstood, deepening their insecure feelings.

Passive-Aggressive Communication

Passive-aggressive communication occurs when someone appears passive and quiet but has a perspective, need, or emotion that is not being expressed directly and instead is expressed obliquely and unclearly. By withholding their experience from others, resentment from repeated unmet needs builds and is expressed indirectly through condescension, undermining, or subtly critical means. This is typically an attempt to express feelings without taking responsibility for them and putting that responsibility on others—this is not typically a conscious motivation, but instead an unhealthy way of coping with a fear of what *could* happen if feelings, needs, or opinions were directly expressed. Passive-aggressive communication can entail:

- Speaking under your breath rather than confronting the person directly

- Suppressing and avoiding anger and resentment

- Offering backhanded compliments (e.g., complimenting while also criticizing)

- Using sarcasm to express dissatisfaction

- Denying there's an issue when there is

- Undermining someone without addressing the issue with them

- Intentionally completing a task poorly to avoid being asked to do it in the future

- Using facial expressions that don't match how you feel

- Making critical remarks or unintended yet hurtful "jabs"

- Appearing cooperative but engaging in sabotage behaviors behind the scenes to annoy others

- Giving others "the silent treatment" (e.g., withholding interaction, avoiding people at the center of the conflict)

Passive-aggressive communication is used to avoid the emotional discomfort of addressing an issue directly with someone. While it may feel satisfying to use spite or other actions to get back at others when hurt or angry, by withholding how they feel, passive-aggressive communicators often feel resentful, misunderstood, and dissatisfied with their relationships. Because others cannot read their minds or know their needs, passive-aggressive communicators' needs and opinions go unmet. In doing so, frustration from others builds, causing serious tension in relationships, ruptures, festering mistrust, and eventually lost relationships. Passive-aggressive communicators may experience frequent guilt and anxiety from repeatedly avoiding the discomfort of being honest with others and self-advocating. This allows low self-esteem to propagate, and is often accompanied by shame, guilt, and frustration that their needs go unmet.

Assertive Communication

Assertive communication entails clearly stating opinions and feelings, and self-advocating without being disrespectful or violating the rights of others. Assertive communicators don't expect others to know how they feel or what they want. They value themselves and are willing to self-advocate while still expressing respect for others. As a result of self-advocating, assertive communicators don't suffer from resentment or pent-up frustration from unmet needs. Relationships between assertive communicators tend to be healthy as well, as others are less likely to guess or attempt to anticipate their needs, because they have already been communicated. Assertive communication looks like:

- Using "I" statements to communicate how you feel, what you'd like, and your unmet needs

- Refraining from blaming others while self-advocating

- Attentively listening without interrupting

- Clearly stating feelings, needs, and wants respectfully and honestly

- Speaking in a calm tone of voice and with a relaxed body posture

- Noticing but not permitting others to manipulate or control you

- Taking responsibility for your impact on others; apologizing and rectifying hurts

- Maintaining good eye contact

- Being willing to compromise and negotiate, and offering to do so when it doesn't infringe on your own rights or needs

Assertive communicators express themselves clearly, allowing others to know where they stand without having to guess. They take responsibility for how they feel and their actions and don't cave in when others try to control or manipulate them. While this approach can be initially uncomfortable to adopt, in the long run, assertiveness allows others to know where they stand.

The productive outcome of this is that others are less anxious to open up to them and interact, as they don't have to worry about outbursts or payback later, facilitating more collaborative, open, and clear communication and healthier relationships. When assertiveness is the main communication approach, it fosters self-esteem and confidence, reduces the likelihood of resentment in relationships, and builds trust.

Let's look at an example of each communication approach. The scenario: Your boss asks you to take on another big project and you're already feeling overwhelmed and having a hard time keeping up with your workload. As additional context, you're experiencing burnout and don't want to work even longer hours.

Passive: Okay, no problem. I'd be happy to help!

Aggressive: I can't believe you think I can take that on! Unbelievable. You know I'm already overwhelmed as it is.

Passive-aggressive: (sarcastically) As if I don't have enough to do already anyway. You got it!

Assertive: I don't currently have the bandwidth for that, but I could revisit this with you in a few weeks when I'll have some big items off my plate. Or if this new project is a higher priority, let's look at what projects we can pause so I can make room for this.

Which one or two styles do you tend to use most often? _____

_____

Which style do you tend to use during difficult interactions? _____

Notice whether the styles you use most often align with or conflict with your values.

Assertiveness is a cornerstone of emotional intelligence and an important communication skill for healthy relationships. Practicing assertiveness requires consistent effort and keeping it top of mind, so it becomes a lifestyle. You communicate verbally, nonverbally, and through your actions. When you live your life according to your values, you are asserting yourself. In that way, assertiveness is also another means of communicating your values to others. It's a building block to living your life according to your values rather than being dictated by your emotions.

Acting As If: Fake It Until You Create It

Strong emotions can captivate us with several reasons to avoid asserting ourselves. The reasons to shirk anticipated conflict could be seemingly endless. When you're not in a position of power, it can be nerve-wracking and intimidating to assert yourself. Or maybe you don't agree with a plan made at work or you've repeatedly felt unappreciated in a close relationship and you're afraid to share it.

As you practice being assertive, make room for the inescapable discomfort that will arise with it. You don't have to feel a certain way before being assertive. Notice whether your mind is stirring up prerequisites to being assertive and let those go. You may not *feel* confident or you may be distracted by low self-esteem or fears of rejection, and that's okay. You can still *act* assertively without waiting for comfortable emotions to accompany it—with practice, your confidence and self-esteem will increase as you assert yourself and your values. This is called acting as if—you act as if you already *are* confident and have self-respect despite the absence of those feelings and assert yourself anyway. If you wait for encouraging feelings to come before trying out assertiveness, they may never arrive. You read that correctly: fake it until you create it. Act assertively over and over again and, with time, the emotions of confidence, self-worth, and self-respect will follow.

Assertiveness Exists on a Spectrum

A common misconception about assertiveness is that it's rude, blunt, or heavy-handed. To the contrary, assertiveness exists on a spectrum, and a skillful assertive approach is custom-made to the person and context of the interaction (e.g., the topic, environment, level of closeness or emotional intimacy in the relationship, nature of the relationship, and cultural factors). Assertiveness can even be playful, particularly when your tone of voice is warm and curious and your ask is nonjudgmental. Next are examples of assertive ways to either start a request or make a clear ask, placed on a spectrum from curious to most direct.

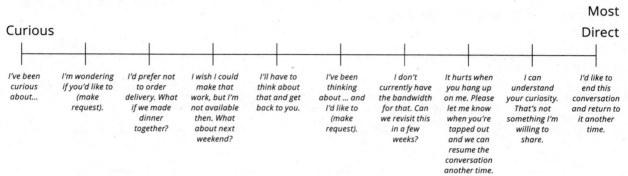

Curious ←————————————————————————————————→ Most Direct

| I've been curious about... | I'm wondering if you'd like to (make request). | I'd prefer not to order delivery. What if we made dinner together? | I wish I could make that work, but I'm not available then. What about next weekend? | I'll have to think about that and get back to you. | I've been thinking about ... and I'd like to (make request). | I don't currently have the bandwidth for that. Can we revisit this in a few weeks? | It hurts when you hang up on me. Please let me know when you're tapped out and we can resume the conversation another time. | I can understand your curiosity. That's not something I'm willing to share. | I'd like to end this conversation and return to it another time. |

Interpersonal Values

Asserting yourself takes concerted practice and commitment. Let's connect assertiveness to your values so they can support you along the way.

Assertiveness Values

Consider why being assertive matters to you. How will being assertive help you live a more values-based life? Returning to the values you identified in chapter 4, look at how assertiveness might help you bring those values to life.

_____

_____

_____

_____

_____

_____

Bring to mind an area of tension in a current relationship that your values would tell you to address. To use assertive communication with this person, what would you have to say and what nonverbal skills would you need to use?

_____

_____

_____

_____

With your values as your guiding light, coupled with the skills you're learning in this book, you'll be well equipped to express yourself more assertively and boost your confidence as you do.

Building Assertiveness

Everyone has different areas of growth with communication, often born out of implied and explicit expectations and learning developed and adopted over time. Using an ineffective approach isn't usually deliberate; it's often a reactive pattern that can be changed with repeated practice and healthy emotion coping. When passive, passive-aggressive, and aggressive communication styles are predominant, they can blind your awareness of just how many daily experiences offer opportunities for assertiveness. This can be addressed by the following practices. Feel free to experiment with them to figure out what helps you build this awareness best.

- At the end of the day, reflect on times you could have asserted yourself, even if in a small way. Let go of any self-criticism; this is simply to build your awareness so in the future you can catch the opportunities in the moment they arise.

- Create a list of where and when you're most deferential to others' either stated or assumed preferences (e.g., do you wait for others to take their preferred seats in a meeting or on a bus before taking yours? Do you refrain from sharing your opinion? Do you say "whatever you want is fine with me" even when you do have a preference?).

- Create a list of situations and contexts that tend to evoke aggressive communication. Then, rehearse emotion surfing of past anger-provoking situations using the Surfing Feelings from the Past exercise (see page 35 in chapter 3). Next, imagine you can return to that interaction and use assertiveness. Create an Assertive Conversation Plan (see page 108) tailored to it. Then, rehearse it aloud, imagining you are back in the anger-provoking situation again. For similar future situations, add them to your Assertiveness Exposure Hierarchy (see following page).

- How do you try to anticipate your perception of others' needs while sacrificing your own? Make a list of what you observe as you ask yourself retroactively at the end of each day how you could have been more assertive. This is not 100 percent problematic, but becomes so when our own needs are consistently sacrificed for others' and we bear the cost of this. This can also be problematic when others reject attempts to anticipate their needs, as it can make them feel frustrated, unseen, or stifled. Anticipating others' needs in a healthy way means your own needs are either still maintained or what is sacrificed is manageable and doesn't prompt future resentment or burnout. Keeping a daily log will help decipher the healthy versus overly self-sacrificing instances.

- Reflect on a relationship you struggle with often. Notice whether recurrent resentment or brooding are emotional fixtures in this relationship for you. Are you often annoyed or hurt, or feel unseen or misunderstood in this relationship? If the answer is yes, this suggests there are some things to assert yourself on. Reflect on your unmet need(s) in the relationship and then make an assertiveness plan (see page 108).

Once you've become more aware of opportunities for assertiveness, you're ready to start seizing them. Because assertiveness is a lifestyle, you can start practicing it in lower-stakes interactions first to build confidence and momentum. If you discover you repeatedly encounter internal barriers applying assertiveness to relationships you're more heavily invested in, start first with those you aren't closely connected to. Return to emotion surfing and emotion coping if you reach emotional overwhelm during exposures, then resume the exposure.

Assertiveness Exposures

Similar to the emotion surfing you learned in chapter 3, you can create opportunities to assert yourself and surf the emotions that doing so evokes. It can be helpful to take a structured, gradual approach by creating what's called an Exposure Hierarchy. An Exposure Hierarchy is a list of situations where you typically avoid asserting yourself or get emotionally hijacked and can't access your assertiveness skills.

Step 1: Create an Assertiveness Exposure Hierarchy

Use the following Assertiveness Exposure Hierarchy to create a very specific list of uncomfortable assertiveness situations. Then, rate how strong you expect the emotional discomfort (including all four components of an emotion) will be on a scale of 0 to 10, with 0 being not at all uncomfortable to 10 being the most uncomfortable. For now, you'll just focus on the first two columns.

If doing the exposures in real life seems too emotionally intense at first, you can modify them by rehearsing your exposure in front of a mirror or recording yourself saying it aloud until the emotions lessen enough that you gain confidence doing it live (see the steps in the following section When Real Life Exposures Are Intimidating). Additionally, you can use the following Assertive Conversation Plan to create and engage in exposure conversations. To get an idea of the specificity a helpful Exposure Hierarchy necessitates, a sample worksheet is included first, and then you can use the blank one to write your own responses (you can also download it at http://www.newharbinger.com/52311).

Assertiveness Exposure Hierarchy

Ali's Example

Assertiveness Exposure	Distress Level (0–10)	Distress Level During Assertiveness Exposure	What I've Learned I Am Capable of Despite My Discomfort
Ask for a raise. 1st exposure: Create Assertive Conversation Plan 2nd exposure: Rehearse and audio record Assertive Conversation Plan; listen to it 3 times 3rd exposure: Have the conversation in real life with my boss	10 6 7	9 4 7	I can self-advocate and justify my value. I realized it's normal to be anxious about these kinds of conversations.
Tell my partner I'd like more physical intimacy in our relationship. 1st exposure: Create Assertive Conversation Plan 2nd exposure: Rehearse and audio record Assertive Conversation Plan 3 times; listen to it and revise if needed 3rd exposure: Have the conversation in real life with my partner	9 7 8	7 4 5	I can talk about sex clearly enough for us to resolve issues, even though it's quite uncomfortable sometimes. Repeating this exposure made it easier to say it assertively.

Assertiveness Exposure	Distress Level (0–10)	Distress Level During Assertiveness Exposure	What I've Learned I Am Capable of Despite My Discomfort
Give my employee constructive feedback at her next annual review. 1st exposure: Create Assertive Conversation Plan 2nd exposure: Rehearse and audio record it at least 3 times. Listen to the best recording. 3rd exposure: Have the conversation in real life with my employee	 9 5 7	 7 3 4	I can be clear and kind while giving feedback directly. This was easier than expected. I revised it once and repeated it 5 times to boost my confidence further.
Inform the team that our marketing approach needs to incorporate TikTok.	8	6	I can share my opinion without being condescending or pushy.
Share my ideas about diversity and inclusion at the next meeting on it. 1st exposure: Create Assertive Conversation Plan 2nd exposure: Share my ideas live during the meeting	 8 6	 6 3	I can stand up for others to be represented. More people were receptive than I expected. I knew what I wanted to say faster than I thought I would.

Assertiveness Exposure	Distress Level (0–10)	Distress Level During Assertiveness Exposure	What I've Learned I Am Capable of Despite My Discomfort
When I'm exhausted, tell my friend who's been struggling that I can't talk on the phone but we can schedule a call for later this week.	8	7	I can protect my self-care needs, even when my emotions scream otherwise. I'd like to repeat this exposure to gain more comfort in it.
Tell Mom, "I'm unable to help today," when I'm too busy, even if she persists and gets aggressive. 1st exposure: Create Assertive Conversation Plan 2nd exposure: Have the conversation in real life	 7 5	 4 3	I can assert myself regardless of Mom being grumpy or rude. I'm proud I didn't yell back at her this time. We scheduled a time that I'm free and won't be overburdened. This was easier to practice than I thought and I felt proud hearing myself say it aloud calmly.
Tell my neighbor, "I'm sorry I can't chat, I have to get going" when she stops me on my way to catch the bus.	6	3	I could quickly decline without getting caught in a long conversation. My neighbor was understanding, which I didn't expect.
Don't apologize when I didn't do anything wrong.	6	3	With repeated practice, this has become second nature. I'm learning I am not responsible for other people's actions.

Assertiveness Exposure	Distress Level (0–10)	Distress Level During Assertiveness Exposure	What I've Learned I Am Capable of Despite My Discomfort
Direct my Lyft driver where to drop me off.	5	3	Even if I feel guilty or like I'm breaking a rule, I can say what works best for me and save myself time.
Tell the restaurant when they made a mistake with my order without being snarky or meek.	5	5	I can politely say what needs to be fixed and it's okay to ask for corrections. I'd like to repeat this the next time it arises.
Ask for the table I prefer at a restaurant.	4	2	I can ask for this and no one seems to bat an eye.

Assertiveness Exposure	Distress Level (0–10)	Distress Level During Assertiveness Exposure	What I've Learned I Am Capable of Despite My Discomfort

Assertiveness Exposure	Distress Level (0–10)	Distress Level During Assertiveness Exposure	What I've Learned I Am Capable of Despite My Discomfort
_____ _____ _____ _____			
_____ _____ _____ _____			

Assertiveness Exposure	Distress Level (0–10)	Distress Level During Assertiveness Exposure	What I've Learned I Am Capable of Despite My Discomfort

Step 2: Gradually Engage in Exposures

Your Assertiveness Exposure Hierarchy is your road map. You'll start at the lowest distress level and gradually work your way up to the highest. During the exposure, use your emotion surfing skills to help you experience the discomfort while still asserting yourself.

After each exposure, check in by adding the highest distress level you experienced during the exposure and list what you learned you're capable of after you completed each. The last two columns are important because they acknowledge hard work and progress, as well as note the distress levels you can withstand, which you may find surprising. It's common to overestimate how distressing something may be or underestimate your ability to get through it. Lastly, celebrating what you're learning you're capable of can help boost your confidence and maintain motivation for future exposures.

Step 3: Repeat

Exposures are most effective when you repeatedly practice them. You'll know you're done practicing a specific exposure when either your distress rating decreases to a 3 or below or you can access your assertiveness skills regardless of your distress level.

Being Assertive in a Specific Relationship

In addition to using an Exposure Hierarchy to structure exposures, focusing on a specific relationship you value can be another approach to increasing assertiveness. Using the following worksheet, you'll reflect on how assertiveness can improve the relationship and practice assertiveness exposures that align with that goal (you can also download it at http://www.newharbin ger.com/52311).

===================== Assertive Conversation Plan =====================

Reflect on a relationship in which you are currently having difficulty asserting yourself. Who is this person in your life and what makes this relationship important to you? Sometimes this answer isn't immediately obvious. For example, let's say you find a coworker difficult to work with. He's often dominating in meetings and isn't open to new ideas to collaborate, even when the projects you're both working on aren't going well. Although he gets on your nerves, if you value your work and career, he's still an important relationship to you at a minimum because improving your working relationship would help you both succeed more at work. Or it may be a meaningful relationship because your values are to be respectful, advocate for your team, and help others, all of which can support you in asserting yourself.

_____

_____

_____

_____

_____

What are one or two goals you have for how you can improve this relationship with assertive communication? Be specific so you know what you're working on and can measure your progress (for example, set a clear boundary of when I'm not available to work in the evenings or tell my teenage son we'll have to strike a compromise on his birthday gift because of our budget constraints).

_____

_____

_____

With your assertiveness goal(s) in mind, what values would you be honoring in this relationship while you work toward those goals? As a quick review, goals can be checked off once and done, whereas values are ongoing things you deeply care about (see chapter 4 for more details).

_____

_____

Combining your values in this relationship and your assertiveness goal(s), write one or two assertive statements you'll need to say to both honor your values and help you meet your goal(s) (for example, "I know you'd like the latest iPhone for your birthday, but unfortunately our budget doesn't allow for that. What else have you been eyeing lately?").

_____

_____

_____

_____

_____

_____

You now have a goal for how to improve a relationship you care about, and you know how you can assert yourself to help achieve that goal. Now that you've made a plan for how you'll assert yourself in this relationship, you can add this to your Exposure Hierarchy. If you'd like to further boost your confidence beforehand, the next section will help you rehearse it.

When Real Life Exposures Are Intimidating

Rehearsing aloud your Assertive Conversation Plan can help you notice and experience emotions it evokes while you continue onward. Just like you'd create a rough draft for a writing project, sometimes rough drafting assertiveness helps you find a genuine and values-aligned voice, easing your ability to have the conversation in real life. If you haven't yet created an Assertive Conversation Plan, choose which item from your Assertiveness Exposure Hierarchy you'd like to rehearse, then write or type how you could assert yourself in that particular situation. Then follow these steps:

1. Find a private place free of distraction and say aloud the assertive statements you wrote in your Assertive Conversation Plan. Notice and let go of any judgment, self-doubt, or self-consciousness.

2. This may provoke emotional discomfort with strong urges. Just notice those and allow them to be there without acting on them.

3. Say the assertive statements aloud at least three times.

4. On a scale of 0 to 10, rate your distress level when you first said them aloud and on the third practice.

5. Now, using a cellphone or computer to audio record yourself, press the record button and practice saying the words aloud again. To help you practice, just focus on capturing the audio. You'll add video in later chapters after you've gained more confidence in these skills.

6. Record yourself saying your assertive statements until saying the words aloud begins to feel more natural and evokes less emotional intensity.

7. Now listen to the last one or two recordings and notice your tone of voice. Is it assertive? An assertive tone of voice is warm and calm; it's not loud, aggressive, or intimidating, nor is it quiet or too difficult to hear. If your tone isn't assertive, practice saying aloud your assertive statements in a calm, steady voice.

8. Rate your distress level from 0 to 10 after the last recording.

9. Lastly, reflect on what you learned you're capable of by doing this practice. Consider how you managed emotional discomfort, resisted avoidance urges, and persisted in saying the words aloud. Also reflect on your use of assertiveness skills.

Assertiveness Practice During Emotional Discomfort

Using your emotion surfing skills in tandem with practicing assertiveness will help you succeed in communicating skillfully with others. You can evoke uncomfortable emotions a few ways, so feel free to experiment to ensure your practice is most useful. The aim is to evoke emotional discomfort at a 5 or higher out of 10 and then, once you're there, to say your assertive statements.

Option 1: Bring to mind the conversation you'd like to have, using the Assertive Conversation Plan as your guide. Close your eyes and imagine you're about to have this conversation. Allow yourself to see where you are, notice the person or people you'll be speaking to, and really take in their faces and the situation. Now say aloud the assertive statements you wrote.

Option 2: Alternatively, bring to mind a challenging and uncomfortable interaction you've had in the past. Ideally this would be the same person you wrote about on the Assertive Conversation Plan. Really see it again, hear it again, and take it in. When your distress level is at a 5 or higher, pause this visualization no matter where you're at in the scene, take a deep breath, and say aloud the assertive statements you wrote.

Option 3: Lastly, with a trusted friend or loved one, ask them to role-play the conversation you'd like to have. Ask them to really take on the communication style and tone of who you'd be speaking to, which may require some coaching from you. As close as possible, you want them to act like how you anticipate this person will be when you have the conversation. As they do this, notice and allow emotional discomfort to build, and when it's at least a 5 or higher, ask them to pause (regardless of where you're at in the role-play) and then say aloud the assertive statements you wrote.

Summary

With your emotion surfing skills at your side and a clear, structured plan to increasingly assert yourself, you'll be well prepared to effectively communicate and improve your relationships as you go. Assertiveness is crucial to emotional intelligence and is a gift to your relationships. It builds trust and facilitates deeper connections as others learn more about your needs, opinions, and perspectives in ways that help their ears stay open and receptive.

CHAPTER 8

Connecting Through Attunement

Several years ago, while walking to work, I was feeling grumpy and gripped by worry about what the day would entail. Serendipitously, I looked up and noticed a woman walking toward me, the sunrise sparkling off the skyline behind her. Struck by the beauty of the orange glow and her warm facial expression, my worry suddenly ceased. As our paths crossed, we both honored this instantaneous moment of attunement and smiled at each other. In this brief exchange, we connected—we chose to lean into the moment mindfully and savor it, leaving us both feeling emotionally seen and appreciated. Still in my memory today, it was a teaching moment of the power that small but deeply felt connections can have. I started my morning feeling isolated and stressed, but left this exchange feeling part of a bigger community, no longer bogged down by the worries of the day.

Attunement is how we express that we are paying full attention to the here and now of an interaction. It is observing and tuning in, akin to the in-the-moment attention required during improv comedy. Or you can think of it like dancing in rhythm with someone—you're noticing cues that inform the steps you take to maintain a feeling of togetherness. Just like learning a new dance with a partner, you may make an attunement misstep or step out of rhythm, but you can readily get back in sync by quickly recovering from mistakes and bringing your attention back to being in the moment with your partner. That is the power of attunement. It doesn't have to be all or nothing or perfect; by using your mindfulness skills, you can re-attune anytime.

Every day there are small and large opportunities for attunement. Relationships thrive when both people feel seen, heard, and valued, despite differences. This holds true regardless of the duration of a relationship or an interaction, from a passing exchange with a cashier at the grocery store to a loved one. To build the relationships you want in all areas of your life and be an expert in emotional intelligence (EI), attunement is a must-have skill.

Attunement Hurdles

Before we dive into this further, let's get real: attunement can be challenging, and the fast-paced world we live in presents quotidian roadblocks. Although we can instantly connect to each other digitally across the globe, ironically, those same capabilities can interrupt and distract us, resulting in increased stress (Yoon et al. 2014), difficulty concentrating (Kushlev, Proulx, and Dunn 2016), and hyperactivity (Kushlev et al. 2016). In addition to the mind's natural tendency to seek distraction or avoid emotional discomfort, cellphones and computers are facilitators of diversion, even during conversations. We use screens to avoid unintentionally and sometimes deliberately. Indeed, research shows we receive an average of over fifty cellphone notifications a day (Pielot, Church, and de Oliveira 2014; Pielot, Vradi, and Park 2018).

But what's the cost of this to human connection in the here and now? It's become commonplace to read texts during a conversation, check Instagram and TikTok at dinner with friends, or digitally "multitask" during meetings. While screen use can certainly be productive, when it's done on automatic pilot, our awareness and connection skills can atrophy and we miss opportunities to have spontaneous, inspiring interactions. In a now outdated poll of American smartphone users, 82 percent said when others use their phone during group interactions, it frequently or occasionally hurts the conversation (Rainie and Zickuhr 2015). Despite this, during the most recent social event they attended, 61 percent of those respondents said they read email or a text, 52 percent took a call, and 30 percent used their phone to intentionally withdraw from the group (Rainie and Zickuhr 2015). Although we have the ease of instantly interacting across the world, we sometimes do so at the expense of connecting with the people right in front of us.

The antidote to this is attunement. Not surprisingly, studies have shown that attunement is a crucial factor for relationship success (Connolly and Sicola 2005; Reid et al. 2007) and it helps romantic partners feel cared for and valued (Greenberg and Goldman 2008). Research has also shown that divorce can be predicted with 87 to 93 percent accuracy, with attunement as a key factor that distinguishes healthy partnerships from ones that end in divorce (Carrère et al. 2000; Gottman and Levenson 2000; Gottman and Levenson 2002).

Misalignments and miscommunication are unavoidable. When we're misaligned, we're alone, as is who we're speaking to. But we can reconnect with attunement to get back in rhythm together and rejoin the conversation. Attuning to others helps us reestablish connection and create new ones. As you sharpen your attunement skills, you'll help prevent misunderstandings, and when they do arise, you'll be equipped to address them effectively without causing continued relationship disrepair.

Attunement Actions

Attunement is flexible in that it can take a lot of forms. The benefit of this is that you can attune in ways that are easier for you and build toward more advanced attunement skills over time as you develop confidence and comfort with it. Attunement is a response to *what's* being shared and *how* it's being shared by the speaker. Attunement actions include:

- Making eye contact

- Using a warm tone of voice

- Matching your rate of speech to your speaking partner's

- Using physical touch to emphasize communication

- Physically mirroring the body language of your speaking partner

- Expressing curiosity in what is being shared

- Using an effective cadence to ask questions

- Shedding happy tears or tears of gratitude

- Reflecting back what you heard

- Validating your speaking partner by apologizing, expressing understanding or agreement, or nodding your head

Let's dig into validation as a form of attunement a bit more. Validation is an expression of understanding and acceptance of another person's point of view and opinion. Even in the face of disagreement, validation is a warm means of recognizing someone's perspective. Validation can sound something like "I hear you," "I can appreciate that," or "I can see why you feel that way."

If attunement sounds hard to grasp or overwhelming, notice those natural thoughts, and let them go. We'll teach you several ways to get attuned and stay in rhythm, even in the midst of a challenging conversation. The skills you've already gleaned in this book will support you along the way. We'll start with the following worksheet (you can also download it at http://www .newharbinger.com/52311).

Attunement Versus Misalignment

Take a few minutes to reflect on the following and see whether you can notice what you may already be doing to express attunement and what some of your stuck areas may be.

How do you already practice attunement? Review the previous list to help you identify attunement actions you already take.

_____

_____

_____

_____

_____

_____

How do you know when you're attuned? What do you notice in your facial expressions, body language, physical sensations, and tone of voice? If needed, think back to the last time you felt a close connection during an interaction.

_____

_____

_____

_____

With whom are you best at being attuned?

_____

_____

With whom or in what situations is it most difficult to be attuned?

_____

_____

What is different about your interactions when you're attuned versus when you're distracted, scattered, or emotionally hijacked?

_____

_____

_____

_____

_____

In completing this worksheet, you may have discovered how you're already using attunement as well as areas for growth. Going forward, acknowledge when you're attuned and give yourself credit for it, and lean into the practice opportunities available to you. You've also noted who you feel most comfortable being attuned with—you can practice new attunement methods with them as a starting place for building confidence and giving yourself permission for the inevitable trial and error of learning new skills.

Giving and Receiving Attunement

To be attuned, you have to express it and receive it through your actions. Sometimes it feels vulnerable to receive attunement, and avoidance urges may arise. This can look like walking away, changing the subject, averting eye contact, or dismissing a conversation. One of the beautiful things about attunement is that it's actionable and can be expressed in small gestures to create meaningful moments. It also doesn't have to take a lot of time. It can be a soft touch for a few seconds to acknowledge expressed appreciation, making eye contact when receiving a compliment, or a warm tone of voice while saying "thank you." Receiving attunement from another is receiving their emotional gift. If it feels overwhelming to receive others' attunement, first focus on expressing it yourself. Once that becomes easier and feels more natural, you can then focus on staying present when others express attunement.

Lead with Attunement Actions and Your Feelings Will Follow

At first, expressing attunement can feel unnatural to those new to it. That's okay. Like a lot of skills, you can first practice expressing it through your actions even if you don't feel the emotions of attunement yet. You read that right: you can phone it in at first. Sometimes phoning it in is the only way to try out a new behavior. Doing so is not disingenuous, as some may fear, because having close, meaningful relationships and effectively communicating are likely the values that drove you to pick up this first book in the first place. Expressing attunement is values-aligned, even if you don't yet feel the emotional connection or intimacy doing so affords. So first, practice attunement behaviors until they become like second nature, and then check in and see whether your emotions have followed suit. Lead first with your actions and your emotions will follow with time.

Building Attunement Skills

There are several ways to practice attunement. Learning how to attune starts with being an active observer: intentionally observing and reflecting on the communication behaviors you see in others without distraction. Below are some tips to help you get the most out of your practice:

- Like the other skills you've learned in this book, set aside time to do them and experiment, even if you notice your mind resisting it.

- Attuning requires present moment awareness. You can set yourself up for success by silencing notifications on your phone, just as you might during an important conversation or meeting.

- There's no one size fits all—give yourself permission to make mistakes and find your own rhythm.

- Attunement skills build with practice. Keep at it until it feels like second nature, then you can proceed to the next chapter.

The following exercises are presented from most accessible and easiest to most difficult. We suggest going in this order and noticing your progress before proceeding to the next exercise. It may be tempting to jump ahead, but sometimes that can be demotivating if you encounter unexpected challenges.

The Attunement Looking Glass

Choose one of your favorite places to watch people interact in person, like a café or a park, or your favorite TV show. Turn off all notifications on your cellphone and computer or turn off the devices completely. Observe the nonverbal communication you see occurring between people using these prompts:

1. First, notice in general their level of eye contact, use of hand gestures, and body language. Are they expressive? Subtle? Stoic or difficult to read? Or something else?

2. Getting more specific, note the different kinds of laughter people express, the intensity of their eye contact, the warmth of their smiles, and the amount of physical space or distance between them.

3. Now, notice whether their eye contact, use of hand gestures, and body language flow in sync with who they're interacting with, even if they are expressed differently. For example, when one person leans forward, does the other do the same? Notice any big differences in how each of them express these nonverbal communication strategies. When they differ, do they appear connected to each other or disconnected?

4. Notice and observe the flow of conversation and their tone of voice. Do they mirror each other? Or are they different but they remain engaged and appear connected?

This exercise is aimed at developing a keener awareness of other people's cues. There are no right or wrong answers. Human beings are complex and dynamic and express themselves in unique ways that can't always be clearly identified. However, when you observe how people respond to each other and their level of connection, you sharpen your attunement observation skills and can identify the styles and patterns of how people in your life tend to express attunement.

Curious Observer

Using the same steps as the previous exercise, observe a loved one's use of eye contact, hand gestures, and body language during a conversation with you. If it's too distracting to notice these during a conversation with you, reflect and identify them after the conversation (as soon after it ends as possible). When you've become adept at recognizing them after the fact, then you'll more readily be able to observe them in the moment.

Learning the unique patterns of how those in your life express attunement will offer opportunities for you to follow suit. For example, your partner, your best friend, and your boss probably have different styles of expressing attunement. As you observe them, you will more readily identify how they communicate being in tune. By learning the steps of their attunement dance, you'll see places where you can join them in rhythm.

Attunement Mirroring

Using your pattern recognition skills, identify a trusted friend or loved one you feel safe practicing attunement with and follow these steps.

1. Reflect on and identify the ways this person commonly expresses attunement.

2. With that in mind, mindfully observe this person during a conversation and begin to model their attunement actions back to them. Being careful not to overdo it, gently share in their communication style. For example, if they tend to make more eye contact than you, practice either making more frequent eye contact or holding your eye contact for just a little longer. Or if they tend to use physical touch to add emphasis to their verbal communication, practice doing the same. This may be softly touching their arm to express care and love, holding their hand, or touching their shoulder.

3. If you feel comfortable receiving feedback, after you've practiced this a few times with the same friend or loved one, ask them whether their connection to you changed as a result of this practice. This can provide invaluable feedback and boost confidence.

Let's Get Digital

Now you'll express attunement again while adjusting your tone of voice. When you're attuned, your tone of voice is thoughtfully modulated to suit the conversation topic, context, and the person you're speaking to. For example, how you speak to loved ones likely differs from the word choices and tone of voice you use during a work meeting or at a doctor's appointment.

Bring to mind a conversation that you expect will be challenging but your values tell you to have. Note who you'll be speaking with, the topic and its emotional valence, and the context.

1. Identify one goal for the conversation. Make sure it is specific and succinct. Focus on just one goal. For example, Ramone's goal in speaking with his boss was "Tell her my team needs one more week to complete the contract negotiation."

2. To assist in achieving that goal, identify the one or two main things you need to communicate. Be specific and succinct, and let your assertiveness skills guide you. Ramone identified "The team has been working hard and encountered some unexpected pushback" and "We have two meetings scheduled to get the information we need. We'll be able to complete the contract next week."

3. Now that you've identified what you'll assertively say and the purpose in doing so, practice saying your assertive statements aloud while audio or video recording yourself on your smartphone, computer, or other audio-recording device.

4. On the first trial run, just notice what your tone of voice and pace of speaking are like before you put more effort into adjusting them. Is your tone direct, warm, cold, or something else? Is your pace slow, fast, or just right?

5. Now again, audio or video record while you practice the main one or two things you plan to say while adjusting your tone of voice and pace of speaking to match the person, context, and topic. Record yourself practicing this three or four times or until it begins to sound natural. Now play the recordings and, with kindness, note whether your tone of voice, pace of speaking, and use of assertiveness are in alignment with the person, context, and topic and facilitate your conversation goal. Make any adjustments necessary and re-record until your delivery matches those needs.

Speaking assertively while using attunement skills requires repeated practice aloud, which at first can sound unwieldy or awkward. That's normal and part of the learning process. Saying it aloud and reviewing your recordings also builds self-awareness, so you can make adjustments on the spot in the future. With consistent practice, you'll be able to modulate your tone and word choices, and succinctly assert yourself in real time. If you find recording it too uncomfortable, start with saying it aloud a few times, and then record it. You will catch more areas of strength and areas for improvement when you hear a recording.

Summary

Attunement means tuning in and expressing that to your listener. When we aren't attuned, it can set the stage for perceived or real misalignment, fostering a ripe environment for miscommunication and feeling unheard or unseen. These experiences create misunderstandings that require more conversations to repair. Small moments offer opportunities to observe and emotionally tune in to who you're interacting with, and it's those small moments that matter and can positively accumulate to build a strong connection, no matter how brief the interaction or who this person is in your life.

CHAPTER 9

Expressing Empathy

In the previous chapter, you learned about attunement and how to express it. In this chapter, we'll build on that by focusing on empathy expression. To recap, attunement communicates "I hear you and I'm with you." Empathy conveys "I feel for you, and I see your pain" and involves connecting with those feelings and expressing them to reassure your listener you care. In this way, empathy expression facilitates a felt sense of connection with others and helps us appreciate others' experience more fully. Similar to attunement, empathy is a balm to misunderstandings and relationship ruptures, allowing us to stay engaged with one another while seeking to understand and resolve issues.

You may have noticed we use the word "expression." Sometimes we *feel* empathy but withhold *expressing* it. This avoidance is understandable, as expressing empathy can feel vulnerable. But it comes at a cost: withholding empathy prevents its beneficial powers from creating and expanding connection when it's needed most. This chapter is aimed at helping you connect with and foster empathy. As you do this, notice any uncomfortable emotions and avoidance urges, surf them, and reconnect with your values related to communication and relationships.

Empathy Is a Necessary Social Skill

So why is expressing empathy worth the emotional discomfort it can evoke? As a highly social and interactive species, empathy expression is socially advantageous. Eons ago, it was required to form cooperative societies, allowing community members to understand collective needs and respond to them. In fact, the absence of empathy could result in disastrous consequences, such as being outcast from the community and premature death. Still today, it is very difficult to form close, meaningful, or lasting relationships when empathy is consistently absent from our interactions. Withholding empathy expression creates a perception that we are aloof, guarded, rude, self-focused, and difficult to engage with, and worse, that we cannot be trusted or seen as safe for others to be open with. Unfortunately, everyone loses when there is a dearth of empathy.

Taking this one step further, when we struggle to express empathy for others, our strained and tense relationships give way to profound loneliness. Despite some prolific myths, loneliness affects adults of all ages (Surkalim et al. 2022) and is associated with increased risk of heart disease, stress, depression, anxiety, suicide, cognitive issues, and premature death (Cacioppo and Hawkley 2009; Prohaska et al. 2020; Surkalim et al. 2022). Data pooled from seventy studies of more than three million people showed that those who are chronically lonely have a 26 percent higher risk of dying sooner than their non-lonely peers (Holt-Lundstad et al. 2015). That's right: being lonely increases your risk of dying sooner.

Our sensitivity to other people's experience is a necessity, not a weakness. Thankfully, we're all born with the capacity to connect and create strong, lasting relationships—our ancestors' survival depended on it and it is a teachable skill with daily opportunities for practice. Especially during difficult conversations, expressing empathy has several benefits, as it:

- Creates emotional intimacy

- Deepens and strengthens feeling connected in a relationship for both parties

- Provides validation and understanding

- Increases emotional intelligence

- Facilitates quicker repair after relationship ruptures

- Builds relationship resilience and helps prevent divorce

Empathy Is Healthy Vulnerability

Having difficulty expressing empathy during challenging interactions is understandable. In the midst of being emotionally hijacked, it can be difficult or seem impossible to notice, let alone express, empathy. Some of our most intense emotions, such as feeling hurt, angry, ashamed, humiliated, defensive, helpless, or frustrated, can be so loud that we can't feel empathy for the person we're interacting with. If we perceive we're under attack, our fight-flight-or-freeze response activates, coupled with emotion urges to self-protect (for example, to withdraw, get defensive, yell, or walk away). Now we're blinded and can't see and recognize the full fallible human being we're interacting with in the moment. With loved ones, sometimes our emotions are so overwhelming, we forget this is a person we respect, admire, or deeply love. By then, we've lost touch with why this person or conversation matters to us at all and focus fully on self-protection, often regardless of the cost. Empathy is an afterthought, and by then, we've already said things we regret and aren't proud of. Does this sound familiar?

We all fall into this trap sometimes. The key is to increase the frequency and speed with which you can access empathy even in the midst of being emotionally hijacked so you can respond in ways that align with your values. The emotion surfing and attunement skills you've already learned can ease your path toward empathy expression. This chapter will teach you some foundational skills for building empathy. While we can't provide a comprehensive menu of practices, the methods offered here, coupled with the attunement practices and emotion surfing, will help you increasingly connect with and express empathy. The next worksheet will help you identify empathy expression in someone you admire (you can also download it at http://www.newharbinger.com/52311).

Empathy Role Model

Bring to mind someone you can open up to with more ease than others. This is someone you trust and who makes you feel safe to be vulnerable with. Close your eyes and, for a couple of minutes, reconnect with times you've felt close, cared for, or connected to this person. Alternatively, you can bring to mind a pet that is responsive to your emotional needs or a TV or movie character that is loving and kind. With this person or animal in mind, answer the questions below.

How does this person use nonverbal communication to engage with you? For example, do they have a quietly curious facial expression when listening to you or do they use touch to emphasize empathy or validation?

_____

_____

_____

_____

What does their nonverbal communication look like when you feel most cared for or connected with this person? For example, do they lean in when talking or smile with a higher inflection in their tone of voice when excited?

_____

_____

Your answers can give you guidance on how you may also want to express empathy. Looking at how positively you experienced this person or animal's empathy, what approaches of theirs do you want to commit to practicing with others?

_____

_____

_____

_____

You now have an empathy expression plan. A note of self-kindness: empathy expression practice may evoke discomfort. That's normal and serves as a reminder of your humanness. Notice any unwanted experiences and allow them to be there; they are signs of growth as you work toward creating a new relationship to yourself and a new approach to interacting with others.

In the following exercise, you'll revisit times in the past you felt emotionally hijacked and didn't notice the opportunity for empathy; this can help you create space to practice empathy now. As you do this exercise, your mind may conjure self-judgment. Just notice that and kindly let it go. We all get emotionally swept up in the moment and miss opportunities for empathy, so everyone can benefit from this practice. Because it can be difficult to notice opportunities for empathy during heated or emotionally intense interactions, reflecting on them after the fact helps you catch them, notice your internal cues of being hijacked, and rehearse empathy skills.

In this exercise, you'll use visualization skills and surf your emotions as you reconnect with your perspective and explore another's during a past painful interaction. This practice is best done in a quiet place where you won't be interrupted and can take between 10 and 20 minutes. You can follow along to a guided audio version of this visualization at http://www.newharbinger.com/52311 or make a recording of this on your cellphone.

Empathic Perspective-Taking

Bring to mind a time in which you felt hurt or wounded by someone and your emotions in that moment were at least a 7 on a scale of 0 to 10. This should also be a time in which you couldn't feel empathy for the person you were interacting with.

Walk yourself through the interaction as if it were a movie, watching it scene by scene. Recall where you were, who you were with, what you could hear, and what was being said. Really connect with as many of your senses as possible.

Notice the emotions this evokes now as they arise. Allow them to be there as they are.

Note the most uncomfortable emotion you're experiencing in this very moment and rate its intensity.

As you reconnect with that emotional pain, ask yourself what kindness you needed most in that moment. What was your unmet need in this interaction? For example, did you want to be heard, understood, validated, respected, appreciated, acknowledged...or something else?

Take a few deep diaphragmatic breaths as you sit with this unmet need. Let go of any judgment or criticisms that arise, of you or the other person.

Now, reconnecting with this challenging interaction, allow yourself to explore any potential unmet needs the person had. Be a curious observer. What was dissatisfying to them about the interaction? What potentially didn't feel good for them in that moment? Allow your emotions to be exactly as they are.

Take a few deep diaphragmatic breaths as you sit with the other person's unmet need. Let go of any judgment or criticisms that arise, of you or the other person.

Now imagine what emotions you'd experience if you had that unmet need. Be curious about the other person's emotional experience. Notice the emotions that arise in you as you do this.

If you notice your mind giving excuses or justifying anyone's behavior, just let those thoughts go. We all bring pain to our interactions with others sometimes, even if we don't intend to. If it helps, you can say to yourself, "We're all doing our best even if that hurts sometimes."

Gently bring your attention back to the breath. Take a few full breaths in and out of your diaphragm. When you feel ready, and only when you feel ready, gently open your eyes.

The following worksheet will help you debrief from the visualization (you can also download it at http://www.newharbinger.com/52311).

Empathy Reflection

In doing the visualization exercise, what new things did you learn about the other person's perspective and their experience of the interaction? What did you discover about what they may have found difficult or dissatisfying in the interaction?

_____

_____

_____

_____

What do you think the other person's unmet needs were? Be as specific as possible.

_____

_____

_____

During the initial interaction, did any of your values feel threatened or at risk? If so, which ones?

_____

_____

_____

When you observe this interaction now more objectively, does it still seem as if those values were threatened or at stake? (It's okay if the answer is yes.)

_____

If you had a time machine and could return to this interaction, how would you honor your values in that moment? (Be careful to notice and let go of any self-judgment.)

_____

_____

_____

_____

Congratulations on doing a challenging exercise and taking the time to reflect on it! Empathy perspective-taking exercises require the courage to self-reflect and explore different ways to engage with difficulties in the future. At the end of the day, we live with ourselves 24/7 and can't escape that—choosing values of self-growth helps make that reality easier to accept and maybe even embrace.

Troubleshooting Empathic Perspective-Taking

If you have difficulty imagining the other person's point of view or experience during challenging interactions, these options might help:

- Cycle through the painful interaction scene a few times before you attempt to imagine the other person's experience. This can help evoke the painful emotions and remind you of the details of the scene, which can lessen the emotional intensity and provide an opening to explore how the other person may have felt.

- Alternatively, do the perspective-taking exercise a few times. Repetition can help you reconnect with the other person's experience. If by the third cycle through the steps you're still having difficulty, skip that scene and practice the exercise with another scene or another person.

- If the interaction you're using for the scene leaves you feeling too emotionally hijacked to access empathy, that's okay. Just choose a lower emotional distress level, aiming for a 4 or 5 out of 10.

- Alternatively, if you're too emotionally hijacked to access empathy, emotion surf it until your distress level reduces to a 5 or below, and then continue the exercise.

- Getting in touch with your five senses as much as possible can help you recall the scene. Once connected to the scene, imagine what the other person's five senses experience might have been. Then continue with the exercise.

Nonverbal Empathy Expression

Empathy can be expressed verbally and nonverbally. We'll focus next on nonverbal expression skills, as they are often the easiest to master and usually provide quicker opportunities to recover if you make a mistake along the way. Mistakes are part of the practice of developing expertise in any skill; allow yourself room to make them without getting caught in self-criticism.

Nonverbal communication makes up most of the messaging we express to others. Although we may be silent in a conversation, we are still always communicating something. Nonverbal communication includes:

- Body language and posture

- Eye contact

- Facial expressions

- Subtle gestures

- Tone of voice

- Physical distance from others

- Touch

These nonverbal methods of communication can be powerful, particularly when used to attune and express empathy.

As with verbal communication, nonverbal skills are most effective when used in response to what's being communicated. They are like an attunement dance. Empathy expression can be tailored to who you're speaking with, the social context, the cultural context, and the topic being discussed. Tailoring empathy expression to these factors takes practice. The following exercise is a good starting place in which the risks of making a mistake don't come at any social cost.

Nonverbal Empathy Expression in a Fictional Setting

In this exercise, you'll practice nonverbal empathy expression while watching a scene from a TV show or movie. This can give you the confidence to practice empathy expression in real life later on.

1. Choose one or two nonverbal communication domains from the previous list that you'd like to practice expressing.

2. Pick a drama TV show or movie you can watch uninterrupted for at least 15 minutes.

3. As you watch, pause the show when a character is expressing emotional distress. In response to their emotional pain, practice how you'd express empathy for them using the one or two domains you identified. It's okay if you're not sure how to do this— just give yourself room to experiment.

4. If the domain you chose to practice doesn't suit the emotional pain or context, keep watching until you find an opportunity that seems well suited for it. If you're not sure, that's okay too. Allow yourself room to experiment with empathy expression in this low-stakes exercise.

5. Notice self-criticism and let it go. Keep practicing even if your emotions and their urges tell you to stop. This practice can feel silly or awkward. Allowing yourself this practice offers low-risk ways to get more comfortable with authentic empathy expression.

Repeat this practice as many times as is needed until your emotional distress level with the chosen domain lessens to below a 4 out of 10 or until your confidence that you can express empathy despite discomfort is at an 8 or higher. In addition to repeating your practice, extending how long you engage in this exercise can help you excel in expressing these empathy skills more quickly. Once you've reached one of those two markers, repeat this practice with the next one or two nonverbal communication domains in which you'd like to hone your skills.

Nonverbal Empathy Expression in Real Life

Now you'll practice what you've been learning during a live conversation with someone. Similar to learning attunement skills, choose a trusted loved one or friend who will be patient and kind as you practice this exercise.

1. Choose one or two nonverbal communication domains you'd like to practice with this person.

2. Ahead of interacting with this person, remind yourself what you're working on so you can keep it top of mind.

3. As you listen to their experience and notice how they express emotions, practice nonverbal empathy expression.

4. After the interaction, ask for the other person's feedback. What did the interaction feel like for them? Did they feel you were empathizing with them?

Repeat this practice as many times as needed until your confidence rating is at least a 7 out 10 (with 10 being the most confident). If there are some nonverbal communication domains you haven't yet practiced, be sure to use this exercise with them as well so you have a variety of ways to express empathy and can tailor your approach to the person, context, and topic in the future. Once you're confident doing this with trusted loved ones and friends, then you can expand it to other appropriate social contexts, such as work or school.

When you feel confident in your ability to express empathy nonverbally despite emotional discomfort that arises, you're ready to begin practicing verbal empathy expression through reflective listening and asking curious questions. The following exercises are best practiced in the order they're presented, as they build in complexity as you increase your skills.

Reflective Listening

Reflective listening is a well-studied communication skill used to aid comprehension, inform your listener that you are fully present, or summarize what's been said to prevent misunderstandings. If you've been in psychotherapy before, you may recognize this skill. Reflective listening is especially useful in preventing and resolving conflict. There are four goals in reflective listening:

1. Obtain clarity on what the speaker is communicating.

2. Reassure your listener you are listening.

3. Help the speaker clarify what they want to express to you.

4. Help the speaker feel understood by you.

Reflective listening can involve interpreting what you believe the speaker has said and asking it as a question to ensure you understood them correctly. It can also entail verbalizing an emotion you hypothesize the speaker is feeling to get feedback on whether you're correct. It's important that reflective listening does not involve judgment or unsolicited advice—both can feel invalidating and thus shut down a speaker, creating relationship ruptures. To be successful in practicing reflective listening, follow these guidelines:

- Listen more than you talk.

- Be attuned to the speaker.

- Respond to the emotions and thoughts being directly expressed, not just the facts in the situation or ideas being presented.

- Rephrase and clarify what the speaker has said.

- Avoid giving advice, expressing criticism or judgment, asking questions, or saying what you feel, believe, or want.

- Use a curious tone of voice, avoiding a tone that sounds harsh, critical, or judgmental.

The two primary techniques for using reflective listening are mirroring and paraphrasing. Mirroring entails repeating key phrases you hear the speaker saying. This could look like replying to "I'm so sick of you being late for dinner" with "I can really appreciate that you're tired of me being late for dinner." Here are some other ways you can start a mirroring sentence:

- What I'm hearing you say is…

- You're wondering if…

- You feel like…

- I can really appreciate that you're feeling…

Paraphrasing, on the other hand, involves repeating a summary version of what you've heard to ensure that it's accurate. Paraphrasing could look like replying to "I'm nervous your report won't be done in time and we'll lose this account. I've been losing sleep over this" with "You're feeling concerned that my report won't be completed on time." Notice that regardless of the technique used, what is being reflected back are thoughts and/or emotions. Once the speaker and listener obtain confirmation they are on the same page about what's been said, you can then decide how else you want to reply to their perspective and feelings, letting your values lead the way. Here are some ways you can start a paraphrasing sentence:

- You're feeling x because…

- What you're struggling with the most is…

- On the one hand you think (or feel) x, and on the other hand you think (or feel) y.

- What's most difficult about this is…

Reflective Listening Practice

In this exercise, you'll reflect back what you hear someone saying during a conversation and do some preparation work to facilitate your success. Be sure to note your observations in a journal or cellphone so you can notice patterns later.

1. Choose one or two reflective listening examples or create your own prior to an interaction you know you'll be having. Choose to practice this skill with a trusted loved one, friend, or colleague whom you know will be kind and nonjudgmental.

2. During a conversation with them, practice your reflective listening statement(s). Notice their response to it and how it impacts the interaction. If it is too difficult to note their response during the conversation, that's okay.

3. Take notes on what you learned from each practice opportunity, including how the other person responded and any key reflective listening phrases you used that had a positive impact on the interaction.

4. Ask for positive feedback on what it felt like to the other person to be listened to in this way. Then, if you are emotionally resourced to receive it, ask for one piece of constructive feedback. Any more than one piece of constructive feedback could be discouraging or result in shutting down, making continued empathy practice more difficult. Make a note of the positive and constructive feedback in your journal or cellphone.

Aim to practice this exercise a few times a week, taking notes on what you learned and how it impacted the interaction. After a couple of weeks of this practice, review your notes and notice the benefits of reflective listening. After practicing it with loved ones and friends, start to practice with those you feel neutral toward, building your confidence further before lastly practicing with those you find difficult or are uncertain how you feel about. Once you feel confident you can use reflective listening with different people and across different contexts, you're ready to add a new empathy skill to your repertoire: asking curious questions.

Asking Curious Questions

Sometimes we don't initially understand someone's emotional pain. Reflective listening can help us obtain more clarity and understanding, but sometimes asking more directly about someone's experience is needed. When this is the case, empathy expression becomes a discovery process of asking careful questions to learn more about the person's experience, opening up opportunities to express empathy. Below are just a handful of examples of how you can ask about someone's experience, deepen your connection to them, and create space to express empathy.

- What has this experience been like for you?

- What do you find is the hardest part?

- What's underneath this difficulty for you?

- What upsets you the most about this?

- If you could change one thing about this (their experience or the situation they find difficult), what would it be?

- What do you notice your mind circles back to the most about this?

- What hurts the most?

- What's one thing you wished other people could understand about this?

- What's been on your mind the most?

- If there were only one thing I understood better about how you're feeling, what would you want it to be?

To practice this skill, you'll follow a similar process as you did in the Reflective Listening Practice.

Curious Listening Practice

In this exercise, you'll curiously ask questions when you aren't sure what someone else is feeling or trying to express to you. Be sure to note your observations in a journal or cellphone so you can notice patterns later.

1. Choose one or two curious question examples from above or create your own prior to an interaction you know you'll be having. Start by practicing this skill with a trusted loved one, friend, or colleague whom you know will be kind and nonjudgmental.

2. During a conversation with them, practice your curious questions. Notice their response and how it impacts the interaction. If it is too difficult to note their response during the conversation, that's okay.

3. Take notes on what you learned from each practice opportunity, including how the other person responded and any key curious questions you used that had a positive impact on the interaction.

4. Ask first for positive feedback on what it felt like to the other person to be listened to in this way. Then, if you are emotionally resourced to receive it, ask for one piece of constructive feedback. Any more than one piece of constructive feedback could be discouraging or result in shutting down, making continued empathy practice more difficult.

Similar to the other practices, repetition can help increase confidence and develop the helpful habit of being a curious listener. Once you feel confident using these skills with loved ones, ask them for more constructive feedback and incorporate that into your practice. Then, you'll be ready to use these skills with people you feel neutral toward, and then, when appropriate, with those you find difficult when the context warrants this kind of understanding. For example, let's say you have a colleague you find is consistently difficult to collaborate with and you're working on creating a marketing plan together. During meetings, they typically express frustration, anxiety, or anger. To foster collaboration, acknowledging their feelings may be imperative. You could ask, "What's the most frustrating part about this for you?" if their primary emotion appears to be frustration. In this way, you can tailor the curious questions to ensure your query is appropriate to the person, situation, and context.

Summary

Empathy is a core social skill built into the fabric of the human species. We all need it, even if sometimes we try to protect ourselves from the vulnerability of it. Have you ever noticed that when you are the least likely to express or notice feelings of empathy is typically when you feel hurt the most? By using your emotion surfing skills, combined with connecting through empathy, you can stay attuned despite emotional pain and deepen your feeling of connection to others. This is all part of practicing emotional intelligence.

## CHAPTER 10

Practicing Emotional Intelligence

You know those clips you see on the news during a hurricane that vividly show the effects of a raging storm? Despite the wind scuffling against the microphone and the visual blur from high winds, you can still see palm trees, standing tall and firm. They're a strong, steady, and reliable presence. Emotional intelligence skills are equivalent to the tough roots palm trees develop. They allow us to stay grounded and communicate with clarity and warmth, even during a difficult or uncomfortable conversation.

Over the last nine chapters, you've grown and watered those strong roots. You've learned the skills of emotional intelligence, and now you're ready to practice them all together, ahead of having a challenging conversation with someone. By rehearsing in advance, you'll set yourself up for success. We'll guide you through a step-by-step process to do that. By the end of this chapter, you'll have created a comprehensive plan for how to have a challenging conversation using the skills you've learned in this workbook.

Step 1: Accept Discomfort

First things first, discomfort will likely show up no matter how hard you try to avoid it. That's okay—it's a reassuring reminder that you are indeed human. So it can be helpful to notice it, make space for it, and give yourself permission to feel it. To preserve your energy for the conversation, you can practice your emotion acceptance skills, including emotion surfing. In the following exercise, you'll name the discomfort you anticipate experiencing so you know where to apply your emotion acceptance skills (you can also download the worksheet at http://www .newharbinger.com/52311).

Willingness to Feel Discomfort

Who are you planning to have this conversation with? _____

Focusing only on the most important things you need to communicate, set one or two goals for the conversation. Make sure your goals are specific, clear, and realistic to achieve in one conversation.

_____

_____

_____

_____

To have this conversation, what discomfort will you need to be willing to experience?

Emotions: _____

_____

Physical sensations: _____

_____

Thoughts: _____

_____

_____

Urges (to avoid or act on): _____

_____

To make space for those experiences and have this conversation, what emotion coping skills will you use before and during the conversation?

_____

_____

_____

Making Space for Discomfort

Now that you know what discomfort might arise, you'll use your emotion surfing and emotion coping skills to help you ride it out. This will not only help you feel better in the moment, but it will have the added benefit of conserving your energy for having a productive conversation.

Avoiding discomfort is an instinctual reaction all humans have. When you're anticipating a conversation that you expect to be difficult, the mind can get overly focused on things you could do to relieve the discomfort. The mind can also be clever in finding reasons to dodge what you think will be challenging. Thankfully, you get to choose how you respond to discomfort and avoidance urges, letting your values guide you. As you prepare for this conversation, it might help to review some worthwhile benefits of feeling uncomfortable.

- When you can name and accept your own emotions, you give yourself space to also notice and connect with someone else's. Suppose you begin to feel angry during a conversation. If you notice this and allow the anger to be there, you're also opening up the possibility that your conversation partner is feeling angry too, and that's okay. Discomfort might show up for both of you. If it does, you can use that experience as a reminder to be kind to yourself and to express empathy and attunement with the other person.

- Discomfort is not always a message that you should refrain from doing something. In fact, it's expected that you'll often feel some discomfort while taking action toward your values. For instance, feeling nervous about giving a presentation doesn't mean that you should not do it! It may just mean that you care a lot about the topic and really hope to connect with the people you're presenting to. Discomfort can be a sign that you're acting on what matters most to you. Put another way, feeling uncomfortable when you're doing something that matters to you can be a signal that you're living your life in a fulfilling way.

- Discomfort is also a healthy reminder that we are humans who feel deeply sometimes. Those feelings can be cues to what we care about, who we care about, and what we want to stand for. In this sense, uncomfortable emotions are a guide that reconnects us with our values.

Step 2: Lead with Your Values

Your values are the things that matter most to you in life. By honoring your values, you'll be able to engage in meaningful actions, even in the face of difficult or painful experiences. To recap what you learned in chapter 4, values are very individual. They are not based on what others expect of you or what you think you *should* be doing. You choose your own values. Keep that in mind before having a difficult conversation, and reflect on *your* values related to the person, social context, cultural context, and topic to be discussed. This can help you stay emotionally grounded and support you in honoring what really matters to you.

Take a few minutes to revisit the values worksheets you completed in chapter 4. Then, with that clarity, look at how your values apply to the specific conversation you want to have. If it's easier, you can flip back and forth from the pages in chapter 4 to the following worksheet (you can also download the worksheet at http://www.newharbinger.com/52311).

A Values-Based Conversation

Who is this person in your life you plan to have a difficult conversation with? Write their name and your relationship to them here (e.g., spouse, mother, boss):

_____

What's important to you about this person in your life?

_____

_____

_____

What's important to you about the topic of conversation or issue you'd like to discuss?

_____

_____

_____

What are the big values having this conversation will honor? (For example: connecting, getting support from others, asserting my needs, helping others, taking accountability.)

_____

_____

_____

_____

Keeping your values in mind can reconnect you with why you're having this conversation in the first place, and it can help you keep moving in the right direction, even if things get difficult. Willingness helps you move your foot from the brake pedal to the gas, and your values tell you which direction to steer.

Step 3: Express Attunement and Empathy

You're aware of the emotions this conversation might bring up for you and the values this conversation will help you honor. Now let's explore how the soft skills of attunement and empathy can help. They are the necessary glue that bonds us to others. Connection will help you turn this challenge into a success.

To briefly recap what you learned in chapters 8 and 9, attunement communicates "I'm here with you, right here, right now," and empathy communicates "I see you and what you're feeling right here, right now."

Have you ever had a call or an interaction with a customer service rep who made you feel great? They were generous in helping you, even if they couldn't provide all of what you wanted. Warmth and kindness can make a huge difference in your experience of a potentially disappointing or frustrating situation. For this reason, emotional gifting can be wonderfully effective in making a difficult talk go as well as possible. What's the positive or even joyful experience you want to leave your conversation partner with after a challenging interaction? Sure, it may be a difficult conversation for both of you, but did you inspire them? Or help them feel seen, understood, or respected by you? These are key elements in conveying attunement and empathy, which you'll explore in the following worksheet (you can also download it at http://www.newharbinger.com/52311).

Expressing Attunement and Empathy

Emotions can be loud and distracting. What can you do to give the other person your undivided attention during the conversation?

_____

_____

_____

Keeping in mind what you know about this person (things they care about, find interesting, or value), what are some ways you can foster connection with them during this conversation you plan to have?

_____

_____

_____

_____

How will you show the other person that you see and hear them with nonverbal communication (tone of voice, body language, facial expressions)? Be specific.

_____

_____

_____

_____

Take a couple of minutes to imagine what it might be like for them to be in this conversation with you. Take a mental note of the emotions they might experience. Notice and ride out any emotions this evokes in you. Now, bringing yourself back to the conversation you'd like to have with this person, what can you say and do to convey attunement and empathy?

_____

_____

_____

_____

_____

By thinking in advance about how you'll convey attunement and empathy, you are setting yourself up for a conversation in which the other person comes away feeling heard and respected, and in which you've accomplished your goals in a way you can feel good about. And you'll be honoring your values to boot.

Step 4: Communicate Skillfully

Now that you have in mind the emotional gifts you want to provide in the conversation, you'll focus just on verbal communication skills. In the next exercise, you'll tailor the Assertive Conversation Place you learned in chapter 7 to this particular context and conversation.

Emotionally Intelligent Assertiveness

This formula provides a step-by-step sequence. When you follow it in this order, you can facilitate openness and connection from the very start of the conversation and clearly express what you want or need.

1. **Express gratitude** for this person in whatever ways are genuine to you. What do they mean to you? What do you appreciate about them? It may simply be that you're grateful they took the time to talk to you. Write one or two sentences that express your gratitude, written as if you were saying them aloud to this person.

    _____

    _____

    _____

2. **Describe your concern objectively**, focusing on just the facts. State clearly and succinctly what your concern is, without judgment, conjecture, hyperbole, or blaming. If it helps, imagine you're standing in front of a judge and presenting the facts. What would you say? If it would help, revisit chapter 7 for a refresher on assertiveness.

    _____

    _____

    _____

3. **Be clear** in how you make your ask. Are you asking for the opportunity to have your perspective heard? Are you asking for a compromise after a disagreement? Is there a boundary you want to enact? Write your ask concisely, ensuring it is stated assertively and aligns with your values and primary goals for having this conversation.

    _____

    _____

    _____

4. **Reflect with openness**, considering the other person's perspective and what feedback or requests they may make of you during this conversation. With that in mind, how can you verbally respond in a way that aligns with your values? For example, if they express feeling hurt or frustrated with you, use your empathy and attunement

skills. If they want you to negotiate or compromise with them, consider how you can respond to their offer. If you're unsure how you feel about a request, you can say something like, "Thanks for sharing that. I want to give this the thought and time it deserves. I'll get back to you."

_____

_____

_____

_____

Now that you've gone through these four steps, you have a strategy for effectively communicating what you want and need while maintaining a good relationship with the other person.

Step 5: Create Your Emotional Intelligence Action Plan

Congratulations! You now have all the elements of your Emotional Intelligence Action Plan. You know how to manage discomfort, you know what values you're honoring in the conversation, and you know what you want to say and how (using assertiveness and the soft skills of attunement and empathy). Let's put it all together in one place so you can more easily see how to act on the plan you just made. You may also find that your thoughts have evolved as you've worked through this chapter. Now you can incorporate any helpful changes. The following worksheet serves as your second draft, with new refinements to set you up for success (you can also download it at http://www.newharbinger.com/52311).

Your Emotional Intelligence Action Plan

For each step below, fill in your answers as you see them now. When you get to step 5, write out verbatim what you can say to the other person. This will help you further rehearse it and notice how it sounds and feels, which may help you fine-tune it.

Step 1: My primary goals for this conversation are:

_____

_____

Step 2: The values I'm honoring by having this conversation and doing so skillfully:

_____

_____

Step 3: If needed, I can reduce emotional intensity that might occur by using these skills:

_____

_____

Step 4: I'll attune to who I'm speaking to by using these verbal and nonverbal skills:

_____

_____

_____

Step 5: I'll start the conversation with gratitude by saying:

_____

_____

Step 6: I'll describe and be clear in what I'm asking for by saying:

_____

_____

_____

_____

Step 7: I'll express empathy by:

_____

_____

Step 8: If I'm not sure how to respond to feedback or requests, I will give myself time to reflect by saying:

_____

_____

_____

_____

There you have it—your Emotional Intelligence Action Plan! Great work putting all the pieces together.

Step 6: Take It for a Test Drive

When you're getting ready to do something that might be difficult, rehearsing ahead of time can go a long way toward boosting your confidence. The Coping Ahead exercise that follows will help you practice carrying out your Emotional Intelligence Action Plan. You can follow along to a guided audio version at http://www.newharbinger.com/52311 or record it on your cellphone.

Simultaneously saying the words aloud, practicing your tone of voice, and using the skills you've learned in this book can help you notice areas where your skills are strong, as well as where you could use more practice. Be kind to yourself as you rehearse. Kindness will help you build your skills and confidence faster than self-criticism would, and it will help you conserve your energy too.

Coping Ahead Visualization

Get into a position that works for you and your body today. Close your eyes if that feels comfortable to you, or softly fix your gaze on the floor. Begin by breathing in and out from your belly. Taking in full, deep breaths, allow your belly to expand. Breathe out fully, allowing your belly to deflate. In and out.

And now bring to mind the plan you made to have a challenging conversation with someone. Imagine yourself in the place where you'll be having this conversation. Really see the surroundings…notice what that space looks like. Notice the other sounds you'd hear there. Notice who else might be there too. Notice and make space for any discomfort you're experiencing as you do this.

Continue to breathe deeply.

And now imagine you could zoom out and see yourself from a bird's-eye view. Watch yourself take the first step in starting this conversation. Really imagine yourself doing it. And now begin to say aloud what you plan to say. Notice any discomfort or unhelpful passengers, and gently let them go.

Being careful not to judge, just notice what it's like to hear yourself say the words aloud.

And now do this again. Watch yourself taking this first step, saying the words aloud. Watch it in as much detail as you can. Really observing yourself, but with kindness.

Make space for any discomfort that arises, allowing it to be there. Now practice continuing on with your plan for the conversation by saying the words aloud and using your attunement and empathy skills. Focus on how you say the words and the body language you use, practicing this now. Watch yourself speak with attunement and empathy.

Notice what it's like to see yourself speak aloud and express attunement and empathy. Just noticing without judgment or criticism.

And now one more time, say aloud with attunement and empathy what you plan to say in this conversation. Kindly watch yourself as you do this, making space for discomfort.

And now allow that image of yourself to fade. Gently return your attention to your breath. Breathe in fully and exhale completely. Notice the rise and fall of your breath. Each time you breathe in, know that you're breathing in. Each time you breathe out, know that you're breathing out. And when you feel ready, and only when you feel ready, gently open your eyes.

Great work! You just took an important step to boost your confidence in having difficult conversations. When you've practiced ahead of time, it can be much easier to enact the plan in real life.

Although it can sometimes be tempting to quickly rush to the next step, it's worthwhile to solidify your practice by taking stock of how you did using the following worksheet (you can also download it at http://www.newharbinger.com/52311). This provides an opportunity to reflect on your achievements, savor them, and acknowledge what you've learned about yourself in the process. Doing so can also help combat the self-doubt or self-criticism that can arise in future situations, and it can remind you of what you're capable of when your mind or emotions might otherwise be skewing the picture. You'll also look at any areas where you'd benefit from more practice. Knowing that will tell you what to focus on in future rehearsals.

Reflecting on the Coping Ahead Visualization

What do you think you did well? Be specific and give yourself credit for the skills you used.

_____

_____

_____

_____

When, if at all, did you notice you had difficulty saying aloud what you planned? How, if at all, did that affect your delivery?

_____

_____

What did you do well in expressing attunement and empathy?

_____

_____

What are some ways you can improve your attunement and empathy expression during this conversation?

_____

_____

_____

How, if applicable, could you be clearer in what you're asking for or otherwise improve your verbal communication?

_____

_____

_____

You've just taken your preparation one step further by honestly taking stock of how you did. Don't hesitate to give yourself credit where credit is due! Be gentle with yourself when noticing areas where you struggled—that's a normal part of the process of learning and practicing new skills.

2

2

Step 7: Record and Review

Imagining yourself having a difficult conversation is a really important step in preparing. Now you're going to take it a step further by making a recording you can review afterward. Hearing yourself practice a conversation can provide powerful and invaluable feedback. It allows you to see and hear your skills in real time and adjust as needed based on that immediate feedback. Experiencing that level of awareness and flexibility will go a long way in honing your emotional intelligence skills. When you can consistently observe how you're doing and make adjustments as needed, you'll be an emotional intelligence expert.

In this step, you'll follow your Emotional Intelligence Action Plan while video or audio recording yourself. If you have a smartphone, use the video record function while propping your phone on a surface. Test out whether your facial expressions and voice are easy to see and hear by recording a few seconds first. Make any adjustments needed. If you don't have a smartphone, you can use a computer to video or audio record or ask a trusted friend or loved one to record you. If they don't have a smartphone or computer either, they can simply observe as you practice and then give clear, constructive feedback on how you did.

Press play to video or audio record and practice following your Emotional Intelligence Action Plan. It's okay if seeing yourself on the screen takes some getting used to. Keep the recording going. You can restart at the beginning of your plan as many times as you need. Then, use the following worksheet to reflect on your performance (you can also download it at http://www.newharbinger.com/52311).

Reflect on Your Recording

1. Review your final take of the video/audio twice, even if you notice urges to avoid this. Reflect on what you did well and where you need to improve.

2. For each item below, mark it if you did well in that area. If it's an area for improvement, leave it blank so you can return to it later.

   ☐ Was your tone of voice warm and open?

   ☐ Did you look up or make eye contact while asking something or asserting yourself?

   ☐ Was the volume of your voice easy to hear throughout the conversation?

☐ Did you stay focused on the top one or two goals for the conversation?

☐ Were you clear in describing your experience?

☐ Did you make your ask concisely, clearly, and assertively (without "beating around the bush")?

☐ Did you use validating or empathic statements?

☐ Did you use attunement skills?

☐ Did you use reflective listening?

☐ Was the pace of your speech easy to follow? Was it too fast or too slow?

☐ Did you honor your values in your verbal and nonverbal communication?

3. List areas for improvement and let go of any self-criticism or judgment that arises. Be specific so you know what to work on.

_____

_____

_____

_____

4. Rate your highest distress level during the conversation, from 0 to 10:

_____

5. Rate your most common distress level during the conversation, from 0 to 10:

_____

Reviewing your own work can bring up a lot of discomfort. Congratulations for embracing that uneasiness and honoring your values along the way! Even if it makes you cringe, hearing and/or watching yourself practice new skills can help you more quickly develop and hone them effectively.

Next Steps

You now have more data on what you're doing well and where to practice next to build your confidence and have difficult conversations in an emotionally intelligent way.

If you're unsure how you did, ask a trusted friend or family member to watch the video or observe you rehearsing the conversation. Or they could role-play it with you, acting like the person you'll be speaking to. Someone who is kind, honest, and an effective communicator can provide important feedback and maybe even reassurance of what you're doing well, and where, if anywhere, you might need to improve.

In deciding whether you're ready to go ahead with the conversation, there is something else to consider, and that is the level of emotional activation you felt during rehearsal. This is where your distress level comes into play. Distress levels can be an important source of information. You can use them to gauge whether you'd benefit from additional practice of the exercises in this chapter or whether you're ready to have the conversation. Here are some guidelines:

If your highest or most frequent distress level was between 7 and 10, did you follow your plan and communicate effectively despite the discomfort? If yes, you're ready to have the conversation. If no, that's totally normal. Practicing your emotion regulation skills before you rehearse the conversation again will help turn down the emotional intensity. Then, practice emotion surfing while imagining having the conversation. Repeat this two-step process until either your distress rating has lowered or you're able to communicate effectively despite it.

If your highest or most frequent distress level was between 4 and 7, did you follow your plan and communicate effectively despite it? If yes, you're ready to have the conversation. If no, that's totally normal. Continue to practice emotion surfing while imagining having the conversation. Another option is to practice your grounding skills before you rehearse the conversation again and emotion surf while practicing the conversation.

If your highest or most frequent distress level was between 0 and 4, did you follow your plan and communicate effectively despite the discomfort? If yes, you're ready to have the conversation. If no, you're emotionally ready and at the same time would benefit from repeated skills practice. Focus on rehearsing the skill areas identified in the checklist you completed earlier.

One thing to keep in mind is that having high distress levels doesn't mean you *aren't* ready to have the conversation. As long as you can honor your plan in rehearsing the conversation regardless of the emotional intensity, you're ready to have this conversation in real life. A higher distress rating just means that practicing emotion surfing and/or emotion regulation skills could help you feel more comfortable or confident in having the conversation.

Notice which items you left unmarked on the previous worksheet. In tandem with your distress ratings, these provide a road map for what to do next. If your results indicate that more practice is needed, use the exercises in this chapter and return to the chapters that correspond to the areas for improvement. Then rehearse the conversation again and complete the reflection worksheet once more to help you gauge whether you're ready to have the conversation. Repeat these steps as many times as needed until you can follow the plan despite your distress level. Notice if you feel discouraged, and practice gently letting that go while returning to your values. Repeated practice is normal and to be expected and will build your confidence along the way.

If your results suggest you're ready to have the conversation, go for it! Know that you have what you need to support you, and your values are right there alongside you.

Summary

You've applied all the skills you've learned throughout this book in preparation for a challenging but worthwhile conversation. In the next chapter, we'll check in and take stock of how it went.

CHAPTER 11

Taking Stock

Arriving at this chapter means you've done a lot of challenging work and probably learned plenty about yourself along the way. Congratulations on choosing over and over again to do the hard work self-improvement requires!

In the previous chapter, you created an Emotional Intelligence Action Plan to guide you in having a difficult conversation. Let's check in and see how that conversation went using the following worksheet (you can also download it at http://www.newharbinger.com/52311). If you notice urges to avoid this, just notice those and let them go—taking stock of how you did is essential to discovering progress and identifying what you'd like to work on next time.

═══ Emotionally Intelligent Conversation Debrief ═══

1. What are you most proud of by having this conversation? Be sure to give yourself credit where credit is due (e.g., I shared my physical intimacy interests for the first time, I asked for a raise assertively, I didn't give in when Dad scoffed at the boundary I asserted).

    _____

    _____

    _____

    _____

2. Reflect back on the challenging conversation and how you approached it. What did you do well? Use the checklist below to identify your skills.

    ☐ Was your tone of voice warm and open?

    ☐ Did you look up or make eye contact while asking something or asserting yourself?

    ☐ Was the volume of your voice easy to hear throughout the conversation?

    ☐ Did you stay focused on the top one or two goals for the conversation?

    ☐ Were you clear in describing your experience?

    ☐ Did you make your ask concisely, clearly, and assertively (without "beating around the bush")?

    ☐ Did you use validating or empathic statements?

    ☐ Did you use attunement skills?

    ☐ Did you use reflective listening?

    ☐ Was the pace of your speech easy to follow? Was it too fast or too slow?

    ☐ Did you honor your values in your verbal and nonverbal communication?

3. What skills did you use to manage uncomfortable emotions? Take note of what helped you cope during this challenging interaction.

    _____

    _____

    _____

4. Identify any areas for improvement you noticed. Be specific so you know what skills to continue practicing.

    _____

    _____

    _____

5. Rate your highest emotional distress level during this conversation, from 0 to 10:

    _____

6. Rate your most common emotional distress level during the conversation, from 0 to 10:

    _____

Celebrating what you've done well and the progress you've made can feel cheesy or vulnerable sometimes. Yet without this, you can miss out on knowing what you do well, leaving a residual feeling of overwhelm that may not be reflective of your actual skill level. For areas of improvement you identified and for any areas of follow-up required after the challenging conversation, return to the corresponding chapters to assist with those skills. For example, if your distress level remained distractingly high or the emotional discomfort was difficult to effectively manage, return to chapters 3, 5, or 6 to rehearse emotion surfing and emotion coping. Or if a follow-up conversation or enforcing a boundary will be necessary, consider returning to chapter 7 to revisit how to express yourself assertively and then complete another Emotional Intelligence Action Plan in chapter 10 to support you in this follow-up conversation.

Reassessing Your Emotional Intelligence Level

Now it's time to reevaluate your emotional intelligence (EI) skills more broadly to note where you've made progress and whether there are any other areas for continued practice. Developing EI requires a dedication to practice while being kind and patient with yourself as you go through the inevitable humility of new learning. But here you are, still embracing that challenge! Use the following worksheet to reassess so you know what path to take next (you can download it at http://www.newharbinger.com/52311).

Emotional Intelligence Assessment

The items in this scale are different ways of dealing with emotions and conflict with others. Do your best to rate each item in terms of how often you've used the strategy or experienced the difficulty over the past three months. Be sure to choose the most accurate answer for you, rather than thinking about how you want to be perceived.

Rate how often the following statements are true for you, where 0 means almost never and 4 means you use this strategy or have this experience very often.

0 ——————— 1 ——————— 2 ——————— 3 ——————— 4

Almost Never   Rarely   Sometimes   Often   Very Often

#	Item	0	1	2	3	4
1	It takes a while for me to recover after having strong negative emotions.					
2	I lose control over my emotions with others and lash out or "blow up."					
3	When I find myself in an argument, I am quiet and/or try to get out of it quickly.					
4	I put in a lot of effort to avoid feeling strong emotions.					
5	Disagreeing with others makes me uncomfortable and anxious, so I avoid it.					
6	I often act on my emotions without thinking; I tend to do what they push me to do.					
7	In an argument, I state my case and focus on winning and not losing ground.					
8	If I feel strong negative emotions, I can feel driven to drink, use drugs, and/or cut or hurt myself in some way.					

#	Item	0	1	2	3	4
9	I have to bring up issues with others immediately even if my emotions are still strong.					
10	I avoid asking for what I want or need from others.					
11	I use nicotine, drugs, or alcohol to help change or numb my emotions or distress.					
12	When I'm upset, my behavior gets out of control.					
13	I ignore my own needs to avoid conflict or being seen in a negative way.					
14	My emotions drive my behavior, even if it means I regret it afterward.					
15	I push to get my position across and focus on convincing others to adopt it.					
16	I avoid feeling uncomfortable emotions as much as possible.					
17	If I feel strong emotions (such as shame or anger), I act in ways that hurt me or get me in trouble.					
18	I explore issues in a disagreement and focus on hearing all sides.					
19	I can communicate effectively despite having strong emotions.					
20	I try to give each person, including myself, time to share their concerns.					
21	I adjust my tone of voice and body language to connect with others.					

#	Item	0	1	2	3	4
22	I avoid creating useless tension and focus on what really matters with people.					
23	I think things through before bringing up an issue with someone.					
24	I'm not afraid of having strong emotions and trust that I can recover from them.					
25	I'm aware of my emotions as I experience them and accept them as they are.					
26	I can experience strong emotions and am skilled in managing them.					
27	I know how to adjust what I'm asking for based on who I'm speaking to.					
28	I notice when my tone of voice or body language changes.					
29	I use cues from others to adjust my communication approach.					
30	I know how to develop rapport quickly with someone I'm not familiar with.					
31	I still carry out my responsibilities even if I'm experiencing strong emotions.					
32	I negotiate with others when there is a disagreement and compromise to try to meet each person's needs, including my own.					

Scoring instructions: Reverse score items 1 to 17 such that 4 becomes 0, 3 becomes 1, 2 stays 2, 1 becomes 3, and 0 becomes 4. Score items 18 to 32 as written. Then, add the total points for each column separately. Next, add the totals for each column together to get the total score. Where does your score fall in the ranges below?

0–40: Your emotions often get the better of you and make communication challenging. It's not unusual to need a review of the skills in this workbook. EI takes time and practice in the wild to hone. Consider going through this workbook from start to finish again and maintaining a dedicated regular practice. You're still right where you need to be, doing the work in this book to help you foster the interactions and relationships you want.

41–82: You have moderate EI skills and sometimes have difficulty with strong emotions, emotion avoidance, and/or communicating effectively in the face of uncomfortable emotions. Reviewing this workbook a second time, or selectively revisiting chapters that reflect where you struggle most, can further support you. Revisiting specific chapters or completing this book twice is normal—there isn't much in life that changes overnight, and using EI in the moment takes time to master.

83–128: You have moderately high to high EI skills. Continue to implement your EI skills in your daily life to further enhance them and ensure they're accessible to you when you're most distressed. EI is a lifestyle after all.

Notice what your total score was when you first completed this measure in chapter 1. How does it compare to your current total score? Also, make note of particular areas in which you've improved by reviewing your responses to each item now versus when you completed this measure in chapter 1.

Emotion-driven behaviors subscale reprinted with permission from the Comprehensive Coping Inventory–55 (CCI–55) (Zurita Ona 2007; Pool 2021).

Summary

Emotional intelligence is a series of skills used as a package to enhance our communication and ability to connect thoughtfully with others. As such, this skill set can last a lifetime when continually practiced. The skills you need are available to you throughout this workbook—embody them in your daily life and savor the connections you create from this empowering work. You've got this and you deserve this.

References

Abdi Sarkami, F., B. Mirzaian, and G. H. Abbasi. 2020. "Comparison of the Effectiveness of Metacognitive Therapy and Emotion Efficacy Therapy on Depression and Self-Care in Non-Clinical Depressed Elderly." *Aging Psychology* 6(3): 269–283.

Aldao, A., S. Nolen-Hoeksema, and S. Schweizer. 2009. "Emotion-Regulation Strategies Across Psychopathology: A Meta-Analytic Review." *Clinical Psychology Review* 30(2): 217–237.

Boersma, K., M. Södermark, H. Hesser, I. K. Flink, B. Gerdle, and S. J. Linton. 2019. "Efficacy of a Transdiagnostic Emotion-Focused Exposure Treatment for Chronic Pain Patients with Comorbid Anxiety and Depression: A Randomized Controlled Trial." *Pain* 160(8): 1708–1718.

Cacioppo, J., and L. C. Hawkley. 2009. "Perceived Social Isolation and Cognition." *Trends in Cognitive Sciences* 13(10): 447–454.

Carrère, S., K. T. Buehlman, J. M. Gottman, J. A. Coan, and L. Ruckstuhl. 2000. "Predicting Marital Stability and Divorce in Newlywed Couples." *Journal of Family Psychology* 14(1): 42–58.

Chawla, N., and B. Ostafin. 2007. "Experiential Avoidance as a Functional Dimensional Approach to Psychopathology: An Empirical Review." *Journal of Clinical Psychology* 63(9): 871–890.

Ciarocchi, J., A. Y. C. Chan, and J. Bajgar. 2001. "Measuring Emotional Intelligence in Adolescents." *Personality and Individual Differences* 31(7): 1105–1119.

Connolly, C. M., and M. K. Sicola. 2005. "Listening to Lesbian Couples: Communication, Competence in Long-Term Relationships." *Journal of GLBT Family Studies: Innovations in Theory, Research, and Practice* 1(2): 143–167.

Ekman, P. 1994. "All Emotions Are Basic." In *The Nature of Emotion: Fundamental Questions*, edited by P. Ekman and R. Davidson, 15–19. New York: Oxford University Press.

Goleman, D. 1995. *Emotional Intelligence: Why It Can Matter More Than IQ*. New York: Bantam Books.

Gottman, J. M., and R. W. Levenson. 2000. "The Timing of Divorce: Predicting When a Couple Will Divorce Over a 14-Year Period." *Journal of Marriage and the Family* 62(3): 737–745.

Gottman, J. M., and R. W. Levenson. 2002. "A Two-Factor Model for Predicting When a Couple Will Divorce: Exploratory Analyses Using 14-Year Longitudinal Data." *Family Process* 41(1): 83–96.

Greenberg, L. S., and R. N. Goldman. 2008. *Emotion-Focused Couples Therapy: The Dynamics of Emotion, Love, and Power*. Washington, DC: American Psychological Association.

Holt-Lunstad, J., T. B. Smith, M. Baker, T. Harris, and D. Stephenson. 2015. "Loneliness and Social Isolation as Risk Factors for Mortality: A Meta-Analytic Review." *Perspectives on Psychological Science* 10(2): 227–237.

Kornfield, J. 1993. *A Path with Heart: A Guide Through the Perils and Promises of Spiritual Life*. New York: Bantam Books.

Kushlev, K., J. Proulx, and E. W. Dunn. 2016. "'Silence Your Phones': Smartphone Notifications Increase Inattention and Hyperactivity Symptoms." In *Proceedings of the 2016 CHI Conference on Human Factors in Computing Systems*, edited by J. Kaye, 1011–1020. New York: Association for Computing Machinery.

Linehan, M. M. 1993. *Cognitive-Behavioral Treatment of Borderline Personality Disorder*. New York: Guilford Press.

Mao, L., L. Huang, and Q. Chen. 2021. "Promoting Resilience and Lower Stress in Nurses and Improving Inpatient Experience Through Emotional Intelligence Training in China: A Randomized Controlled Trial." *Nurse Education Today* 107: 105–130.

Martins, A., N. Ramalho, and E. Morin. 2010. "A Comprehensive Meta-Analysis of the Relationship Between Emotional Intelligence and Health." *Personality and Individual Differences* 49(6): 554–564.

Mattingly, V., and K. Kraiger. 2019. "Can Emotional Intelligence Be Trained? A Meta-Analytical Investigation." *Human Resource Management Review* 29(2): 140–155.

McKay, M., M. Davis, and P. Fanning. 2021. *Thoughts and Feelings: Taking Control of Your Moods and Your Life*. 5th ed. Oakland, CA: New Harbinger Publications.

McKay, M., and A. West. 2016. *Emotion Efficacy Therapy: A Brief, Exposure-Based Treatment for Emotion Regulation Integrating ACT and DBT.* Oakland, CA: Context Press.

O'Boyle, E. H., R. H. Humphrey, J. M. Pollack, T. H. Hawver, and P. A. Story. 2011. "The Relation Between Emotional Intelligence and Job Performance: A Meta-Analysis." *Journal of Organizational Behavior* 32(5): 788–818.

Pielot, M., K. Church, and R. de Oliveira. 2014. "An In-Situ Study of Mobile Phone Notifications." In *Proceedings of the 16th International Conference on Human-Computer Interaction with Mobile Devices and Services*, edited by A. Quigley, S. Diamond, P. Irani, and S. Subramanian, 233–242. New York: Association for Computing Machinery.

Pielot, M., A. Vradi, and S. Park. 2018. "Dismissed! A Detailed Exploration of How Mobile Phone Users Handle Push Notifications." In *Proceedings of the 20th International Conference on Human-Computer Interaction with Mobile Devices and Services*, edited by L. Baillie and N. Oliver, 1–11. New York: Association for Computing Machinery.

Pool, E. S. 2021. "The CCI–55: An Updated Assessment Tool for Transdiagnostic Treatment." PhD diss., The Wright Institute, Berkeley, CA.

Prohaska, T., V. Burholt, A. Burns, J. Golden, L. Hawkley, B. Lawlor, G. Leavey, et al. 2020. "Consensus Statement: Loneliness in Older Adults, the 21st Century Social Determinant of Health?" *BMJ Open* 10(8): e034967.

Purdon, C. 1999. "Thought Suppression and Psychopathology." *Behaviour Research and Therapy* 37(11): 1029–1054.

Rainie, L., and K. Zickuhr. 2015. "Americans' Views on Mobile Etiquette." *Pew Research Center*, August 26. http://www.pewinternet.org/2015/08/26/americans-views-on-mobile-etiquette.

Reid, D. W., E. J. Dalton, K. Laderoute, F. K. Doell, and T. Nguyen. 2007. "Therapeutically Induced Changes in Couple Identity: The Role of We-ness and Interpersonal Processing in Relationship Satisfaction." *Genetic, Social, and General Psychology Monographs* 132(2): 241–284.

Sauer, S. E., and R. A. Baer. 2009. "Responding to Negative Internal Experience: Relationships Between Acceptance and Change-Based Approaches and Psychological Adjustment." *Journal of Psychopathology and Behavioral Assessment* 31(4): 378–386.

Schutte, N. S., J. M. Malouff, E. B. Thorsteinsson, N. Bhullar, and S. E. Rooke. 2007. "A Meta-Analytic Investigation of the Relationship Between Emotional Intelligence and Health." *Personality and Individual Differences* 42(6): 921–933.

Selby, E. A., M. D. Anestis, and T. E. Joiner. 2008. "Understanding the Relationship Between Emotional and Behavioral Dysregulation: Emotional Cascades." *Behaviour Research and Therapy* 46(5): 593–611.

Sluyter, D. J., and P. Salovey, eds. 1997. *Emotional Development and Emotional Intelligence: Educational Implications.* New York: Basic Books.

Surkalim, D. L., M. Luo, R. Eres, K. Gebel, J. van Buskirk, A. Bauman, and D. Ding. 2022. "The Prevalence of Loneliness Across 113 Countries: Systematic Review and Meta-Analysis." *BMJ* 376: e067068.

Sutton-Smolin, M. 2019. "Effectiveness of a Transdiagnostic Treatment for Low Emotion Efficacy." PhD diss., The Wright Institute, Berkeley, CA.

Vashist, R., K. Singh, and S. Sharma. 2018. "Emotional Intelligence and Its Relationship with Conflict Management and Occupational Stress: A Meta-Analysis." *Pacific Business Review International* 11(4): 30–38.

Wegner, D. M., D. J. Schneider, S. R. Carter, and T. L. White. 1987. "Paradoxical Effects of Thought Suppression." *Journal of Personality and Social Psychology* 53(1): 5–13.

Wong, C., and K. S. Law. 2002. "The Effects of Leader and Follower Emotional Intelligence on Performance and Attitude: An Exploratory Study." *The Leadership Quarterly* 13(3): 243–274.

Yoon, S., S. Lee, J. Lee, and K. Lee. 2014. "Understanding Notification Stress of Smartphone Messenger App." In *Proceedings of the Extended Abstracts of the 32nd Annual ACM Conference on Human Factors in Computing Systems*, edited by M. Jones, 1735–1740. New York: Association for Computing Machinery.

Zareie Faskhudi, B., A. Karbalaee Mohammed Meigouni, H. Rezabakhsh, and L. Ghelichi. 2021. "Comparison of the Effect of Unified Transdiagnostic Treatment from Emotional Disorders and Emotion Efficacy Therapy on Emotion Regulation Among Adults with Stuttering." *Journal of Applied Psychological Research* 12(2): 185–209.

Zurita Ona, P. E. 2007. "Development and Validation of a Comprehensive Coping Inventory." PhD diss., The Wright Institute, Berkeley, CA.

Stephanie Catella, PsyD, is a clinical psychologist with expertise in transdiagnostic cognitive behavioral therapy (CBT) for trauma, anxiety, and building emotional intelligence. After completing fellowships at the San Francisco VA and the University of California, San Francisco; she codirected the Berkeley Cognitive Behavioral Therapy clinic with Matthew McKay. In addition to her private practice, she authored an FDA-cleared prescription digital therapeutic for fibromyalgia, and serves as an advisor to HealthTech companies.

Matthew McKay, PhD, is a professor at the Wright Institute in Berkeley, CA. He has authored and coauthored numerous books, including *The Dialectical Behavior Therapy Skills Workbook*, *Self-Esteem*, and *Couple Skills*, which have sold more than a million copies combined. He received his PhD in clinical psychology from the California School of Professional Psychology, and specializes in the cognitive behavioral treatment of anxiety and depression.

Foreword writer **Robyn D. Walser, PhD**, is director of TL Consultation and Psychological Services, and codirector of Bay Area Trauma Recovery Clinical Services. She works at the National Center for PTSD; is assistant clinical professor in the department of psychology at the University of California, Berkeley; and has authored and coauthored several books, including *Learning ACT* and *The Heart of ACT*.

Real change *is* possible

For more than forty-five years, New Harbinger has published proven-effective self-help books and pioneering workbooks to help readers of all ages and backgrounds improve mental health and well-being, and achieve lasting personal growth. In addition, our spirituality books offer profound guidance for deepening awareness and cultivating healing, self-discovery, and fulfillment.

Founded by psychologist Matthew McKay and Patrick Fanning, New Harbinger is proud to be an independent, employee-owned company. Our books reflect our core values of integrity, innovation, commitment, sustainability, compassion, and trust. Written by leaders in the field and recommended by therapists worldwide, New Harbinger books are practical, accessible, and provide real tools for real change.

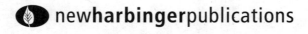 **newharbinger**publications

MORE BOOKS from
NEW HARBINGER PUBLICATIONS

DISENTANGLING FROM EMOTIONALLY IMMATURE PEOPLE

Avoid Emotional Traps, Stand Up for Your Self, and Transform Your Relationships as an Adult Child of Emotionally Immature Parents

978-1648481512 / US $21.95

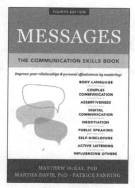

MESSAGES, FOURTH EDITION

The Communication Skills Book

978-1684031719 / US $21.95

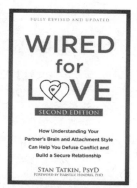

WIRED FOR LOVE, SECOND EDITION

How Understanding Your Partner's Brain and Attachment Style Can Help You Defuse Conflict and Build a Secure Relationship

978-1648482960 / US $19.95

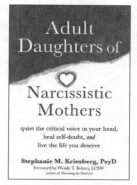

ADULT DAUGHTERS OF NARCISSISTIC MOTHERS

Quiet the Critical Voice in Your Head, Heal Self-Doubt, and Live the Life You Deserve

978-1648480096 / US $18.95

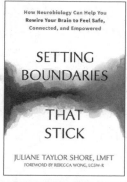

SETTING BOUNDARIES THAT STICK

How Neurobiology Can Help You Rewire Your Brain to Feel Safe, Connected, and Empowered

978-1648481291 / US $18.95

THE HIGHLY SENSITIVE PERSON'S GUIDE TO DEALING WITH TOXIC PEOPLE

How to Reclaim Your Power from Narcissists and Other Manipulators

978-1684035304 / US $18.95

newharbingerpublications

1-800-748-6273 / newharbinger.com

(VISA, MC, AMEX / prices subject to change without notice)

Follow Us

Did you know there are **free tools** you can download for this book?

Free tools are things like **worksheets, guided meditation exercises**, and **more** that will help you get the most out of your book.

You can download free tools for this book— whether you bought or borrowed it, in any format, from any source—from the New Harbinger website. All you need is a NewHarbinger.com account. Just use the URL provided in this book to view the free tools that are available for it. Then, click on the "download" button for the free tool you want, and follow the prompts that appear to log in to your NewHarbinger.com account and download the material.

You can also save the free tools for this book to your **Free Tools Library** so you can access them again anytime, just by logging in to your account! Just look for this button on the book's free tools page.

+ Save this to my free tools library